To: Nathan Love: Mom
Christm...

My Father's WORLD

ISBN 978-1-936208-01-2

LAYOUT AND COVER DESIGN:
Lydia Zook

EDITOR:
Kristy Wadsworth

FRONT COVER STORK PHOTO:
©Torsten Karock/istockphoto.com

Printed in China
Print Management by HeuleGordon, Inc.
Grand Rapids, MI

PUBLISHED BY:
TGS International
P.O. Box 355
Berlin, Ohio 44610 USA
Phone: 330·893·4828
Fax: 330·893·2305
www.tgsinternational.com

My Father's WORLD

AUTHOR

Pablo Yoder

PHOTOGRAPHER

Jacinto Yoder

TABLE OF CONTENTS

DEDICATION

To my son Kenny, the littlest nature lover I've ever known. I love you, son!

THIS IS MY FATHER'S WORLD

FRANKLIN L. SHEPPARD

This is my Father's world, and to my list'ning ears,
All nature sings, and 'round me rings
The music of the spheres.
This is my Father's world; I rest me in the thought
Of rocks and trees, of skies and seas;
His hand the wonders wrought.

This is my Father's world; the birds their carols raise;
The morning light, the lily white
Declare their Maker's praise.
This is my Father's world; He shines in all that's fair;
In the rustling grass I hear Him pass,
He speaks to me ev'rywhere.

This is my Father's world; oh, let me ne'er forget
That though the wrong seems oft so strong,
God is the Ruler yet.
This is my Father's world; the battle is not done;
Jesus who died shall be satisfied,
And earth and heaven be one.

INTRODUCTION

Today God is sitting on His throne in heaven. He is surrounded with great glory, and many, many celestial beings are praising him.

Now imagine that God suddenly opens a small window. His keen eyes look way, way down until He sees Earth. He gazes upon that blue and green sphere hanging down there on nothing and He smiles. He thinks back six thousand years and remembers those six special days when He made His world.

Then God looks closer. He sees His rivers bubbling toward His oceans. He observes His trees and His grasses waving in His wind. He enjoys His dainty orchids and His colorful flowers sprinkled over His gardens. He even notices His charming green moss. He watches His butterflies and His birds flying around in His world. God glimpses His monkeys scrambling through His trees. He is happy with what He sees. He smiles again.

Then God sees something very special bouncing across one of His meadows. He leans forward on His throne to get a better look. What He sees makes His heart swell. This special creature of His is running and skipping like one of His fawns. But it isn't a fawn. It is swinging its arms and singing. Then it trips and falls, laughing, into His grasses. God smiles a very big smile. He even chuckles as He sees the child lying there in His grass, giggling.

The child God sees is you. His child.

You lie there looking up into the sky, and you say, "I wish I could see what's on the other side of that cloud. I wish I could fly past it and see the Father!"

The kind Father hears your request. He looks down and answers, "No. You can't come up here to see me yet. The time will come when all my dear children will be with me forever. But not yet. Even so, my dear child, I do want you to see me. And I have provided a very special way for you to do just that. Today. Would you like that?"

"Yes! Yes!"

"Stand to your feet, my child. Look around you. Do you see my rivers bubbling toward my ocean? Do you observe my trees and my grasses waving in my wind? Do you enjoy my dainty orchids and my colorful flowers sprinkled over my gardens? Have you noticed my charming green moss? Come watch my butterflies and my birds flying around in my world. Catch a glimpse of my monkeys scrambling through my trees. Be happy with what you see. Though they are mine, I also made them for you. Because when you see the world I made, in a special way, you see me.

"Do you remember what I wrote to you in my special Book? I told you that when you see what I made, you learn about me."

The heavens declare
the glory of God;
and the firmament
sheweth his handiwork.
—Psalm 19:1

"My dear child, you can know about me, your Father, by seeing what I made!"

You are one of God's special children. Today, through this book, you are going to learn about Him by seeing the world He made. You will marvel as you observe His creativity. You will be awed as you sense His power. You will be surprised as you realize His intelligence. You will be amazed as you glimpse His knack for beauty. You will be blessed as you feel His tender love. And you will even be tickled as you see His sense of humor.

THE DRY BRANCH
That Blinked

THOU ART the God
that doest wonders.

PSALM 77:14

Chapter 1

THE DRY BRANCH
That Blinked

I wish you and I were in Belize this morning, down by the mission house in Isabella Bank. I would take you to see a bird called the northern potoo, *Nyctibius jamaicensis*. We would walk a mile down the white sandy road until we arrived at a typical Belizean farm. We'd stop at the house, hail the owners, and ask for permission to see the potoo in their corral. A bird in a corral? Just wait and you will see!

Just a lovely Belizean tree, that's all.

We would walk toward the corral, and the first thing we'd see is a huge, green tree standing right in the middle. As we gazed at the tree, Willie, our native guide, would ask, "Can you see a bird a little bigger than a blue jay in that tree?"

You would look and look and see absolutely nothing. Finally you would give up. "There is no bird in that tree!" you'd declare.

"Let's get closer," Willie would suggest.

Then we would walk right under the tree and you would continue to stare at the branches, one by one. But you'd see nothing that resembles a bird. "What color is it?" you would ask, perplexed.

Is there a bird or isn't there?

"It's a brown bird, with darker brown and black markings and little specks of white. Actually, it's very much the color of the tree's bark. That's why you can't see it."

"I can't believe there is such a bird in this tree," you would insist, almost peeved.

"Climb up here on this corral fence with me," I'd suggest, grinning. "Do you see that dead stub stick-

Baby is learning to hold perfectly still.

ing up that makes a fork on that branch? Watch it a little while."

You would stare at the dead stub and then exclaim, "I can see the stick's feathers rippling in the breeze! It sure enough is a bird. I have never seen anything like it! It just sits there, holding perfectly still, sticking its head straight up into the sky."

"I had never seen anything like it, either," I'd answer. "But recently I was here and Willie showed me this wonder bird. That's why I wanted to bring you to see it this morning."

"But why does the bird sit there and just point its beak up into the sky?"

"It's what I call the most perfect camouflage. God gave these birds the instinct to find a dry branch to perch on during the day. The potoo sits that way so he looks like a continuation of the dry stick. Who in the world could find him there?"

"When does he eat if he sits there all day?"

"They are night birds. During the day they close their eyes and sleep, as you can see. But nights they are awake and fly around in the woods watching for insects. If you happen to be there with a flashlight, you can see them sitting upright on branches with their big, owl-like eyes shining bright orange in the light. If you have patience, you can watch as they dart out like flycatchers and catch insects. Insects are their main diet."

"But why is this one sitting in that fork instead of on the end of a dry branch?"

"This bird has a special secret. Do you notice a little white cluster of feathers by her side?"

"Oh yes! Is it her baby?"

"It sure is. Mama bird laid a single, creamy egg with lavender spots in that fork. Then she sat on it every day, pretending she was a fork on the branch. Now her little baby is growing fast. All night long she flies around and brings food for him. Meanwhile he learns to sit still by himself. Isn't he cute? Just a little puff of white and gray feathers."

"How did Willie find this bird?"

"Willie has exceptionally good eyes for things like this. He spends a lot of time in the woods hunting. He enjoys watching nature, and his eyes are trained to see unique things. He comes past this tree every day on his way to the mission where he works. One day he noticed this queer fork and watched it. He also saw the feathers ripple, and maybe he saw it blink."

"What did the potoo do when you were here the last time?"

"At first she just sat there sticking her head straight up toward heaven. But then we got a ladder to get some close-up photos. I placed the ladder right here on the corral fence and climbed up very slowly from behind her so as not to scare her. I didn't think she even found out I was there. I was sure she was fast asleep. But when I saw my photos, I noticed that her head had swiveled around. Her beak was not straight up anymore. Her head had turned to watch me."

"But how could she watch you if her eyes were shut?"

"That's what made me laugh so hard when I saw the photo. She was peeping at me all the time!"

"Well, I'd say that's quite the bird! Thanks so much for bringing me to see it!"

"Yes, this bird is remarkable. I think it's amazing how God gave this bird such a unique, perfect hiding ability. Isn't God simply marvelous?"

You'd better Belize it!

Hey, Mama, are you peeping?

LITTLE Green
hitchhiker

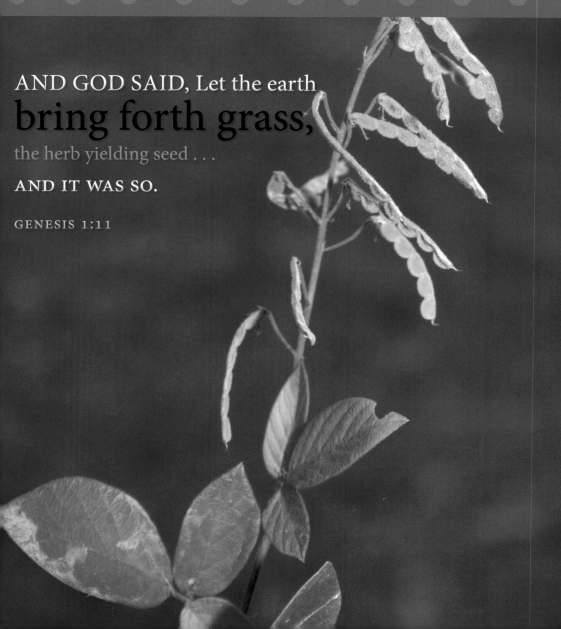

AND GOD SAID, Let the earth
bring forth grass,
the herb yielding seed . . .

AND IT WAS SO.

GENESIS 1:11

Chapter 2

Little Green hitchhiker

Once upon a time there was a little burr growing on his mama plant. He was an important burr. His scientific name was *Desmodium incanum*. His skin was smooth and slick. He was ripening and knew that if he fell to the ground, he would land at the foot of the plant beside his seventy-two brothers and sisters. He also knew that they would all germinate and grow in a pile. He felt sure he wouldn't survive. His bigger brothers and sisters would grow faster than he,

Little Burr with his brothers and sisters on this stem.

choking him out. He knew he really didn't have a chance if he fell off there. So he did some powerful thinking.

"I need to get out of here. I need to get away so I can grow on some faraway turf where there is not so much competition. I desperately need some means of transportation."

So Little Burr said:

"I don't enjoy flying. It's too scary.

"I don't have enough money to buy a car, or even a bicycle, or even to pay a bus fare.

"I don't have legs to walk.

"I can't swim; there is no water.

"I know what. I will hitchhike! But how can I catch a ride?"

Then Little Burr remembered some stuff called Velcro that he'd seen at Wal-Mart. "If I could get some Velcro, I would dress up, and I could catch a ride!" he exclaimed.

So Little Burr ordered some Velcro from Wal-Mart. He was a Central American burr, so it took a long time for the Velcro to arrive. UPS didn't deliver all the way to his plant, so he used snail mail. He was so worried that it would not get there in time. What if he would fall at his mama's feet! On the very day that he felt his grip weakening on the stem he'd been born on, the Velcro arrived. He quickly wrapped himself in it and prayed that some hairy traveler would come around soon.

Just before he slid to his certain death, a dog came trotting along with his sideways gait. As he slipped past, he brushed

> **Just before he slid to his certain death, a dog came trotting along with his sideways gait.**

Nature's best Velcro.
. . . .
Dog tails make excellent transportation.

against Little Burr, who gripped onto the dog's tail. With a happy sigh he cheered, "I am a hitchhiker at last!"

One month later Little Burr was as ripe as ripe could be. His Velcro was much worn now. He was losing his grip fast. But that didn't matter. He was in a faraway place where there was no competition with his seventy-two brothers and sisters. He happily slid to the ground and dedicated the rest of his energies to sprouting into a new plant.

Sure enough, it rained, and Little Burr sprouted and grew into a brand new plant. Eventually he bloomed, and a whole new batch of baby burrs was born, all naturally covered with Velcro!

Then one day Little Burr heard a voice. The voice said, "Hey, here is a nice burr

plant. It's got baby burrs. Just what we need for our photos."

Little Burr looked up and saw a man and his son. They had a fancy camera.

. . . .

Do you believe that yarn? Whoa! Never! I don't either! Well then, let me ask you a tough question. If it did not happen that way, how did it happen? See, some people just insist that God didn't make the world and the burrs. If He didn't, then who did? And how did Little Burr get his Velcro padding? What would the poor burrs have done for transportation all those millions of years before Velcro evolved?

I don't believe in evolution. I believe God planned it all just the way the little green hitchhiker needed it. And I believe it's been that way ever since God made the burr six thousand years ago.

Have you ever gotten your pants or dress full of burrs? I sure have! They are a mess. I've even had some of the little fellows go to church with me. When I get to church and see my pant legs, I groan, "Oh, no! Now what?"

Then I find something to scrape them off. After getting rid of them, I sigh, "That's better." But I hardly think of what I really did. I just gave the hitchhikers a ride. A necessary ride. I helped the burrs find new turf to grow on.

After I get rid of the little stickers, they kind of dry up. Then the janitor sweeps

Uh-oh! Burrs on my pant leg. A pain for me—a ride for him.

them off the sidewalks and into the grass. That's why in Nicaragua sometimes you can find burr plants in the church yard.

If you ever wonder why burrs are so widespread, you'll know it is because Little Burr is so smart, right? Nope! It's the Creator who's smart. Little Burr is just a common little burr. Jehovah is the only one who could come up with something so intelligent and so efficient. And so dandy! "Happy ride, hitchhiker friend!"

THE BIRD THAT'S AS
Tall as You Are

REMEMBER HIS marvelous works
that he hath done.

PSALM 105:5

Chapter 3

THE BIRD THAT'S AS
Tall as You Are

My family and I were in Scotland Halfmoon, Belize, for a week of meetings. While we were there, we got a lunch invitation to Stephen Schrock's home at the nearby Isabella Bank Mission. The person who told us about the invitation added, "By the way, they want you to come with at least three extra hours. They want to take you to the boonies to see some big stork's nest."

I really like invitations like that. See, I love to study birds and am always excited about seeing something new. I also knew Stephen and his family were amateur ornithologists (people who study birds) like myself. I knew something special was in the making.

Several days later we headed for Isabella Bank. My ornithologist blood was bubbling, and I was raring to go. As we ate a quick lunch, Stephen told me about a jabiru stork *(Jabiru mycteria)* nest they had found way up high in a pine tree. The nest, he claimed, held two chicks that already had feathers and were almost as big as the mama bird.

"How long ago did you see those birds?" I asked.

"About two weeks ago."

My heart fell. I was sure that if the babies had feathers and were almost as big as the mama bird, then they would certainly have flown away by now. But Stephen insisted that we try. Maybe, just maybe, they would still be there.

Before long we were geared and ready to go. Stephen crawled onto a big four-wheeler with Kenny, myself, and one of his boys. Willie, the native man who worked at the mission, drove the other jalopy of a machine. It took a while to get the other rig running, and I felt a few misgivings about trying a boonie trip with a contraption so old my grandfather might have ridden it. But he loaded my two daughters on the back and away we went.

As we sped down the dirt road, I leaned forward and yelled into Stephen's ear over and above the roar of the machine, "How far is it?"

"Oh, it takes about an hour to drive it."

"How did you find the nest?"

"Willie was out hunting and saw it from far off. He took us to see it."

Willie, I soon learned, had a special knack for seeing things in the out-of-

doors. His eyes were almost as sharp as a hawk's. He and nature seemed one. Every time I popped a question at him about nature, he had an answer.

We continued roaring down the white, sandy road. Suddenly we hit a trail that just disappeared into the grasses. The two four-wheelers took to the terrain easily, and we entered an interesting world of palmetto palms and grasses. It was so different from anything I had ever seen. This was the Belizean outback, and I loved it instantly.

As the minutes ticked into an hour, I grew concerned. The jalopy had already stopped running several times. Sure, Stephen was a mechanic, and he always got it going again. But sometimes even a mechanic reaches his limit. The sun was terribly hot. We were swallowing what seemed like pounds of dust, and our mouths were parched with thirst. I was concerned that the birds would be gone and this entire safari would be useless. Even if the birds were there, the four-wheeler would surely give out. I'd miss the meeting that evening. And I was supposed to preach the message! And what if we got lost? We buzzed through all kinds of territory. Gnarled oak shrubbery. Palmetto forests. But my fears grew when we entered a huge expanse of grass. I would have gotten lost after the first mile. But Willie and Stephen seemed to know where they were going, so I tried to relax and hung on like a monkey in a windstorm.

Far in the distance we saw some pine trees hugging the horizon. My heart sank when I heard Stephen yell, "The nest is over there in those pines." I thought it might take another hour to get anywhere close. But those four-wheelers kept on rolling, and in ten minutes we were standing on solid ground, downing cup after cup of cold water from the marvelous thermos Stephen had remembered to bring along.

"Pablo," Stephen suggested, "we should leave the vehicles here so as to not scare the birds. You and Willie walk ahead. We will come along behind. Willie will tell you once you get close."

I quickly got my camera gear ready: binoculars, telephoto lens, and tripod. Willie whispered to me as we walked along. "We'll skirt this pine grove, and as soon as we get out into the grasses, you start taking pictures. They are very wary and fly away fast."

Sure enough, on top of a tall pine tree rested a huge stick nest, much like a bald eagle's, only bigger. My heart skipped a beat when I saw three big birds standing on their nest like kings. Through my binoculars I could see that two were adults and one was a baby. The adults were mainly white, and the baby was covered with a brownish sheen. The baby was as big as his mama, and since one baby had apparently already left the nest, this one could probably fly too.

We skirted the pine woods, trying our best not to be seen. I knew we were still too far away for really good photos, but I also knew that I had to start shooting. They could fly away at any moment.

I hid behind a bush and started to take pictures.

I walked another fifty yards, and one parent just neatly stepped off the nest and then, stretching out his long neck, flew in a straight line for the horizon. I snapped several more pictures.

I tiptoed another fifty yards, always trying to stay behind some brush. Then the other parent flew off just as the first one had. The baby was left alone in the nest.

Just as I was ready to try fifty more yards, the baby stepped off the nest too. But he was not as skilled in the air as his parents. It looked as if he were falling. And he was, but clumsily he got his wings in order and began flapping. He flew lower than Papa and Mama, but he flew nonetheless, slowly, in a straight line, neck stretched out, straight for the horizon.

The jabiru storks were gone. But my heart was full. I had seen enough of these

Daddy flew and only Mama and the baby were left.

"Goodbye, baby stork!"

elegant birds to satisfy my ornithologist thirst. "Awesome" was a mild expression for what I had just experienced.

We all walked up to the tree and got a close look at the huge nest. Was it six feet across? I didn't climb the tree to measure it, but it sure seemed big. At the Belize City zoo they told us that that year they had documented only eighteen stork nests. I was glad that I knew there were nineteen, and the best one, I was sure, they had never found!

The jabiru stork is a remarkable bird found from Mexico to Peru. We saw several close up in the zoo several days later. The most astounding thing about this stork is its size. A normal jabiru stork will stand almost five feet tall. That's taller than many of you readers. Jabiru storks have wingspans of up to eight feet. Their bodies are white, with ugly black necks and heads, much like black vultures. They have reddish bands around their necks—a bright red bandanna to add a little color. Their beaks are quite impressive— long, black, and sharp. They are even turned up at the tip, giv- ing the stork a little "nose in the air" look.

Jabiru storks feed in freshwater swamps, marshes, and ponds. They walk along in the water slowly, watching for any living creature lurking there. As soon as they see a poor, hapless minnow, they stab at the water and gulp down the prey. They eat reptiles, fish, and amphibians, including young caimans and turtles.

The jabiru stork at the zoo was vicious. We stood above him on a balcony. He kept

looking up at us as if he were friendly. But watch out! He jumped up into the air. Re- member, he stands almost five feet tall. Then he snapped at us. The zookeeper told us what happens if the rascal gets a piece of human flesh in his beak. We kept our guard up after that, and I concluded that the jabiru stork can be a very aggressive bird.

Didn't our Father go all out making an in- teresting assortment of birds for us to enjoy? I have met and studied many birds in my life. But few gave me the thrill that the jabiru stork did that day in the flat Belizean outback. And through this great stork, I caught a glimpse of the creativity of our great God.

SOMEONE HAS
Been Here!

BEHOLD, GOD IS MIGHTY . . .
in strength and wisdom.

JOB 36:5

Chapter 4

SOMEONE HAS Been Here!

Today, my dear friend, you and I are going to pretend we are on an exploration expedition in the jungles of Brazil. We have long since left all civilization behind. We haven't seen another soul for several days. We don't expect to see another human being for a whole week. There's just no one around this far back in the jungle.

We are walking on a rocky beach beside a rushing stream at the bottom of a wooded ravine. Up ahead we see a lovely waterfall. Hundreds of rocks are scattered all along the river's edge.

Suddenly we notice a set of rocks arranged in a neat circle. Seven rocks in a perfect circle, spaced evenly.

We stare at the circle of rocks in amazement. Funny shivers run up and down our spines. Goosebumps pop out on our arms, and the hair on the back of our necks sticks straight up. Then with wide, questioning eyes we look long at each other. Next we look all around us and peer into the jungle along the river. Then you whisper to me in a hoarse voice, "Someone has been here!"

I nod, my eyes still large, wondering who placed those rocks beside the river's edge.

. . . .

Let's drop the imaginary story. It was exciting, wasn't it? But it wasn't true anyway.

Now let me ask you several questions. "How did we know so surely that someone had been there by the riverside?"

"Because of the circle of seven well-spaced rocks."

"But the beach was full of rocks, wasn't it? There were hundreds of rocks. The last time the river got high, couldn't the current have just washed them into a circle? When the high water went down, there were those seven nicely spaced rocks . . ."

"No. Currents can never space them exactly right."

"You are right, my friend. It takes intelligence to space seven rocks in an orderly, perfectly spaced circle!"

Let's do an experiment. Get a tin can and fill it with pebbles. Sit down on the sidewalk and dump the pebbles on the cement. Did any of the pebbles line up in an orderly fashion? None did, right? But

The graceful fern's scientific name is *Niphidium crassifolium.*

Everything looks natural and undisturbed.

Someone has been here . . .

"Someone has been here . . ."

try it again. And again. Hey, if you have lots of time, do it all afternoon. Did the pebbles ever land in a nice, neat circle, perfectly spaced one from another? No, they didn't, did they? Okay, if you have lots of time, try doing it for a week. Or better yet, for a month. Dumping pebbles from your tin can and picking them up again will never bring order. Nope, there will be no tingles up and down your spine.

No goosebumps. There was no one there. Just a whole bunch of pebbles strewn out on your sidewalk with no order at all. Never. Not even in millions of years.

. . . .

Now let's quit dumping pebbles on the sidewalk. It's too boring, isn't it? Come with me on a walk in my orchid garden. It could be a real thrill if you travel all the way to Waslala, Nicaragua, where I live. Do you see all my orchids? Aren't they lovely? But turn your attention from the orchids for a moment. I want you to notice this plant. It's called the graceful fern.

Look underneath its green leaves. Do you see what I see? Wow!

We stare in amazement at row after row of brown spots. Neat rows on either side of the midrib. Each row has approximately nine little brown dots, or caches of spores,

> **Funny shivers run up and down our spines. Goosebumps pop out on our arms. And the hair on our necks sticks straight up.**

where the leaf is widest. As the leaf narrows toward the tip, the spores' caches are fewer. Eight. Seven. Six. Five. Four. Three. Two . . .

Funny shivers run up and down our

spines. Goosebumps pop out on our arms. And the hair on the back of our necks sticks straight up. Then with wide, questioning eyes we look long at each other. Next we look all around us and peer into the bushes in my orchid garden. Then you whisper to me in a hoarse voice, "Someone has been here!"

You are exactly right! Someone was here. Who was it? That's the question today. Who put those little spores in perfectly spaced rows?

Did the plant itself count the rows and space the dots? Plants don't have brains or intelligence. No, it was not the plant.

Did you line up the spores?

No.

I didn't either.

Was it the President?

No.

Was it Albert Einstein?

No.

Was it Bill Gates?

No.

Was it evolution? No. We already proved that time and chance can never bring order. And yet someone gave order to the graceful fern. Neat, concise order.

Well then, who placed the spores on the graceful fern plant's leaves? It was someone who can count, add, and subtract. It was someone who can make straight rows. It was someone very intelligent. It was our Creator God!

The main reason I know it was God is because His book, the Bible, says He made everything in six days. I believe in the proven book of the ages.

The other reason I know it was God is because there is no one else left. If we are honest and we run over the list of possibilities, a list as long as you want to make it, there is absolutely no one else who could have done it. Just God our Creator is left. And that is enough.

Nature is full of order. Why does an ear of corn always have an even number of rows? (If you don't believe it, go check.) If the earth and the objects up in the sky—the moon and the planets—all zoom around the sun, why don't they ever collide?

Our God is a God of order. Wherever we see order, we know someone was there. And it always was the Creator! Ask me how I can be so sure He exists and I will tell you that, as I look at my own body, I see intricate design and order. Millions and millions of tiny cells, all arranged perfectly and working together. I know it was all planned even before I was born. And as I look, I exclaim, "Someone has been here!"

Little Black
SAMBO

FOR BY HIM
were all things created.

COLOSSIANS 1:16

One day in the life of Little Black SAMBO

Little Black Sambo woke up slowly. The sun was just peeping over the horizon, and its soft heat tickled the fuzzy, black fur on Little Black Sambo's back. He yawned a whopping wake-up yawn. It was time to get up.

Little Black Sambo, a baby black howler monkey *(Alouatta palliata),* was rolled in a tight ball in the fork of a branch high in the guaba* tree. He stretched and unwrapped out of his rolled-up sleeping position. He was ready for action.

Just as Little Black Sambo unwound, a happy-go-lucky hummingbird zoomed past, gathering the sweet nectar from the frizzy, snow-white guaba flowers. Happy-Go-Lucky had a big surprise when, right out from under his cluster of flowers, a comical, black face peered up at him. The hummingbird hovered above Little Black Sambo for just a split second and then zoomed away in high gear. Little Black Sambo just barked a little grunt that meant, "Good riddance!"

Little Black Sambo was thinking a cheerful thought as he jumped from the lowest guaba branch onto the highest branch of the smaller cacao tree. He scooted on down to the ground, his tail always hanging on for safety's sake. Bouncing into the grass, Little Black Sambo began his amble from the orchard to the house where lived the family he loved. He was thinking of coffee, just like his master. He knew his master would be in his office with his Bible on his lap and a cup of delicious coffee in his hand.

Squeezing through the bars of the office window, Little Black Sambo sensed he was welcome. His master kindly picked him up, and Little Black Sambo embraced his big hand and wrapped his ever-handy tail around his wrist. Then his master held him to his warm chest, chuckling and telling his favorite pet all kinds of sweet secrets. But Little Black Sambo kept staring at his master's cup of coffee.

Laughing, his master got up, taking Little Black Sambo along, to find a plate in the kitchen. Then he broke a slice of bread onto the plate. Next he sprinkled a pinch of sugar onto the bread and poured on

* Pronunciation guide for Spanish words and phrases can be found on page 147.

> **He closed his eyes and anybody would have thought he was sleeping. But he was remembering.**

a little bit of milk. Last, but not least, he added a spurt of rich, black coffee. Then he took the plate, placed it on the floor beside his chair, and sat down again.

Little Black Sambo released his master's hand and began to eat his special breakfast. Between bites he sometimes crawled up onto his master's lap and sat

there chewing. This made his master chuckle every time.

After his tummy was popping full, he crawled up onto his master's shoulder. He made purring sounds and licked his ear lobe. His master always snickered because it tickled so much. He knew this was Little Black Sambo's way of saying,

"Thank you!"

The sun was up strong now. Little Black Sambo felt chilly in the house. He'd been cold ever since he got up. Though Little Black Sambo didn't know it, God had built a little solar panel into his body. A black howler monkey's diet consists mostly of leaves, though he also eats fruits and flowers. Because most leaves have little food value, their diet often doesn't produce enough energy. So God made a way to save energy.

Right after his breakfast, Little Black Sambo knew he needed sunlight, so he left his master's comfy lap and lay out on the sidewalk in the sunlight. He closed his eyes and anybody would have thought he was sleeping. But he was remembering.

Little Black Sambo was remembering the time he got lost and found all in the same day. He had lived with his mama in the jungles of Yaró with a troop of about fifteen monkeys. Little Black Sambo had spent most of his first four months hanging onto his mama's back. He had clutched at her fuzzy fur with all four feet and wrapped his ever-handy tail around hers as a sure anchor. Big King, the daddy monkey, had always been the boss. Little Black Sambo was afraid of Big King, especially when he howled many times a day. Big King made the jungle shake when he howled. His voice carried for miles. Little Black Sambo always trembled when Big King howled.

When Little Black Sambo was four months old, he began to crawl off his mama's back to play while she sunbathed in the morning. He played with the other little monkeys his size, jumping around in the branches. Though he still nursed, he learned to eat leaves by licking off scraps from his mama's mouth when she chewed. He was becoming a big monkey, or so he thought.

One day Big King decided that the whole troop of monkeys needed new feeding grounds. Nutritious leaves had grown scarce in their small jungle. To get to a larger jungle, they would have to cross a road. Big King knew that people, those odd folks with no tails, traveled on these roads at times. He waited until he thought no people were coming. Then he took the lead, scooting down the tree closest to the trail. Barking low, grunting commands, he crawled over the grassy area and then across the dirt road. Black howler monkeys are not fast and agile like most monkeys. They have a heavy, slow crawl, like an old, hunchbacked man. It took the monkey troop about fifteen minutes to cross the road. Little Black Sambo's mother was the last in the bunch.

Suddenly the great roar of a truck coming around the corner terrified the whole monkey troop. All the monkeys galloped clumsily for refuge. Little Black Sambo's mother ran with the rest. Just before she got to the road, she crashed down into the ditch and slammed into a rock. Little Black Sambo lost his grip. As his mama jumped up and leaped for the road, Little Black Sambo was flung off her back and plopped into the high grasses. To his despair, his mama didn't stop or look back.

Little Black Sambo crawled out of the grass, blinking, and scampered over the road to follow his mama. He had barely crossed when the huge truck roared to a stop and a little boy dashed out after him. Young hands grabbed him. Little Black Sambo bit them savagely. The boy flung him back into the grass and grabbed him from behind. In no time at all they had carried him away, the young boy holding him tight in the back of the huge passenger truck. The sounds and smells confronting him were all very strange. Little Black Sambo was terrified, but all he could do was hang onto the hand that had found him and hope for the best.

The boy who had caught Little Black Sambo tied a string to his neck so he wouldn't run away. All the boy fed him was ripe bananas. Little Black Sambo had never eaten a banana before, but he was hungry enough to eat them anyway. He missed his mama, her milk, and the leaves he'd been eating lately. He was very lonely and missed the rest of the monkey troop too. Even Big King.

After five sad days of captivity, the little boy who had caught Little Black Sambo took him to a nice house covered with ivy. The little boy talked with a friendly man who reminded Little Black Sambo of Big King. The friendly man had a bunch of small children who reminded him of his siblings. They jumped up and down and smiled as they pointed at Little Black Sambo. His new master took Little Black Sambo into his arms and gave the boy several dollars. The boy left, smiling.

Now, a month later, Little Black Sambo was very happy. He hardly missed his mama and Big King anymore. He was adopted into this new family, and he belonged!

Little Black Sambo ambled off toward the orchard again. He was so glad that his new master understood his food needs. Although Little Black Sambo loved his coffee soup for breakfast, his master knew he really needed leaves to live. Lots of leaves! He also knew that the only one who knew which leaves were the best for his diet was Little Black Sambo himself. That's why, when Little Black Sambo had first arrived at the farm, his master had taken him on leaf finding hunts every morning after his sunbath. Little Black Sambo would cling to his hand while his master held him up to every leaf in the orchard, or so it seemed.

Little Black Sambo knew where to go for lunch!

Little Black Sambo also learned to like bananas. He'd stop by the bananas at our bird feeders on his way to the orchard.

MY FATHER'S WORLD

Here his solar panel is working at full power.

His master knew that the good Lord had put a strange and wonderful thing into Little Black Sambo's taste buds that would tell him when the leaf was just right. He knew exactly when to grab and chow. But if the leaf wasn't right, Little Black Sambo rejected it. If it was poisonous, he knew how to wrinkle up his comical, black face at his master as if saying, "No way, José!"

Now Little Black Sambo had developed his own little leaf route through the orchard. He always started at the foot of the mango tree where his favorite plant hung. He had long since stripped his master's wife's two potted plants she kept on the windowsill. After eating several leaves as an appetizer, he bumbled on down the path toward the cacao grove. For several hours he climbed from tree to tree, choosing the right leaves.

No one can explain how black howlers do it, but not only do they choose the best leaves, they choose the best time to eat them. Some leaves they eat young and tender. Other leaves they don't touch until they are old and tough. Some scientists studied which leaves the black howlers eat and when. They discovered that they always choose them when they have the most protein. God gave them that mysterious inner feeling called instinct. That's what taught them how to be such amazing dieticians.

In the late afternoon Little Black Sambo was sunbathing again on the topmost branches of his guaba tree. His solar panel was absorbing energy for the long, wet Nicaraguan night ahead.

Way down below the high guaba branches, Little Black Sambo heard footsteps. He held perfectly still and listened. Then he heard his master call, "Little Black Sambo." In one wild, reckless leap he jumped into the cacao treetop. He scooted down the trunk of the tree in about fourth gear. He wrapped himself around his master's hand and purred as he held him to his face. He felt his master's little kisses on the top of his head and heard him whispering sweet nothings into his fuzzy ears.

After carrying Little Black Sambo around as he did his chores, his master fed him a tangerine. Then he returned him to the cacao grove at dusk. "Goodnight, baby," his master whispered. He knew that even though Little Black Sambo was only eight months old, he would sleep better out in the woods on the high branches of his favorite guaba tree. Even if the wind blew or it rained, Little Black Sambo was happier up there in a tight ball, swaying in the wind, than he would be trapped in a cage. Also, his master knew that tomorrow would come fast for Little Black Sambo. His heavenly Father would watch over him just as he would watch over his master and his little ones until morning light. Then Little Black Sambo would be back for a coffee breakfast, and a new day would begin for both of them.

Sambo, my friend!

Tiny, Spiny Farmers

GO TO THE ANT . . .

consider her ways,

and be wise.

PROVERBS 6:6

Chapter 6

TINY, SPINY *Farmers*

Today I want to tell you about leaf cutting ants. But first I want to tell you about Bernard.

Many, many years ago a farmer named Bernard Warkentin stood on the deck of a big ship. He was traveling from Russia to the United States. As he looked out over the great ocean he had to cross, he remembered the precious parcels among his luggage. Down in the hold, among his things, he had packed several bushels of wheat seed. It was a special kind called turkey red that grew so well in the Crimea, which was part of Russia. Now Bernard smiled as he whispered to himself, "When I get to the United States, I am going to raise some of the best wheat there is! Turkey red!"

And he did. Bernard moved to Halstead, Kansas, and there he planted his precious turkey red wheat seed. And it did grow well. Not only that, but its fame spread, and soon all the Mennonites were planting the superior turkey red wheat. For the next sixty years the wonderful turkey red became the most planted wheat in all Kansas and the surrounding states. Even today wheat growers say, "Thank you, Bernard!"

But what do Bernard and turkey red wheat have to do with leaf cutter ants? Have patience and you will see!

When we moved to Costa Rica, I was just ten years old. I had a quick eye to see

A troop of leaf cutter ants on their trail.

new things in that strange land. We hadn't lived there long before I noticed little ant trails across the countryside. The trails were cleared of all weeds and grass, like miniature highways. And though I didn't know it, they were just that!

All along the trail I would watch hordes of red, spiny ants rushing along. I soon discovered that all the ants going one way traveled empty, but the ones going the other way all carried a green umbrella. On my hands and knees, I soon figured out what was going on. The loaded ones were carrying little pieces of leaves toward their home. The empty ones were heading to some distant spot to cut and haul in more leaves.

The leaf cutter ants (*Atta cephalotes*) especially like orange tree leaves. Close to our house we had several trees. One day I noticed that something was stripping one of the trees. All along one side of the orange tree trunk ran a row of hundreds of ants. The loaded ones were coming down the tree, carrying their tall, green loads. The empty ones were going up the tree, ready to find and cut up some more leaves. In three days' time the tree was totally stripped of its leaves.

I climbed the tree carefully and found a place where they were actually cutting off the leaf pieces. I watched amazed as each tiny ant found his leaf and then neatly trimmed off a round piece. I especially admired their scissors.

Many years later, when I had children of my own, we visited a grove of jungle trees close to where we lived at the time. I knew of a huge ant colony in this jungle, so I took my children along to study it.

Among the huge jungle trees were mound after mound of red-brown dirt where the ants had dug out their homes. Each mound had a hole in the center which was the entrance to the underground maze of tunnels and rooms. We watched how the worker ants hauled out tiny clods of dirt, and we shook our heads in amazement to think that they had moved all those big mounds of dirt out of their den, piece by tiny piece.

We counted all the active highways entering the ant city that could easily have housed five million ants. There were thirteen main highways into this huge ant complex. Each highway had thousands of ants bringing in what I used to think was their food. As we followed the highways away from the nest, many of these freeways branched off in different directions in the jungle. So there was actually a whole network of interstates and roads across this piece of jungle.

"Watch this," I told my children. Then I took my machete and whacked the earth next to the mound again and again with the flat side. Soon hordes of larger, meaner ants poured out of each hole. "These," I explained, "are the soldier ants that guard the nest. They don't work at all; they just come bite you when you mess with them. Watch out!"

Back in Costa Rica, I had always thought that the ants ate the leaves they hauled home. But since then I have learned that they don't. There is a mystery here that we need to solve. What are the leaves for? They sure use a lot of them daily! Now here is where Bernard Warkentin comes in.

Once an ant colony gets too big, it sends out a swarm, much like honeybees and other insects do. But these ants only send out queens and males. Both the males and the females can fly at this stage. They fly up into the sky just before dawn. The males catch the females and mate with them in the air. The males then die, and the queens fly far away, return to the ground, drop their wings forever, and find the perfect place to start a new colony. Each queen digs a tunnel six to eight inches straight down into the earth and hides at the bottom of the shaft.

As she rests down in the bottom of her well, she smiles to herself and whispers, "When I get my garden started, I am going to raise some of the best wheat—oops! I mean fungus—there is!"

The queen has some precious seed hidden too. Not in her luggage, but in her mouth. The queen has a special pocket in her mouth where she hid a tiny start of the wonderful fungi she collected from her former home before leaving. Now she gets it out and starts cultivating it. She does this with some leaves she cuts herself and mixes with her own liquid manure. Then she "plants" the fungus in this gook. This makes a great garden. If the fungus gets lost at this stage, the queen dies. She cannot find any more of the precious substance, and the new colony must have it to survive.

After the queen's garden is growing, she lays some worker eggs on the pile of fungus. For the next four to five weeks, the queen waits until her babies are born. As soon as the new workers hatch, they take care of her first and then tend to the fungus garden. As more and more hatch out, they open the tunnel bigger and start add-

No, they don't carry their scissors in their apron pockets; they carry them in their mouths. Their sharp mandibles are made just right to cut leaves.

Efficient little earthmovers!

If you want to experience nature, let one of the soldiers get you!

See the little minima riding on the leaf? The little minimas get a ride because everybody knows how hard they work!

that make wonderful mulch for the now flourishing garden. They mix the pellets with their saliva and manure and make large mats with it. The fungus is then planted on these mats. The fungus itself is light colored, almost white. The spores grow all through the mat, and the mat becomes a white, spongy, bread-like cake.

The fungus then produces swollen hyphae, which are the ants' main food source. The tiny minimas tend to all the gardening and feed all the other castes, hand to mouth, including the queen.

Once the ant colony is all set up and running smoothly, every ant is happy. There is work for all. Everyone does his part. By the way, the little minimas also ride along with the media ants when they bring in the leaves. They watch out for a parasitic insect called the phorid fly that drops maggots onto the passing ants. The minimas warn the media ants of danger when the flies come close.

The queen lays eggs. The soldiers make sure everybody is safe. The medias haul leaves for the garden. And the minimas tend the gardens and bring food for all. Do you think someone remembers to thank the queen, like folks today thank Bernard, for remembering to bring the little batch of seed along? I hope that even today all the tiny, spiny farmers say in ant language, "Thank you, Queen!"

But most important, shouldn't we all be thanking God for coming up with such an incredible world? Shouldn't we be bubbling over with praise to such a wise and great God who takes care of us?

Say to God, "How awesome are your works!"

ing on rooms. At the same time they start bringing in leaves.

The leaf cutter ants live by castes, different sizes doing different jobs. The queen and the males are the biggest of the cutter ants. Their sole purpose is reproduction. Next are the soldiers, who are also whoppers. They run around on the trails or stand watch at the colony entrances. The next caste, smaller ants called media workers, haul all the leaves. When the medias bring in the leaf pieces, they drop them into one of the chambers. Then the smallest ant caste takes over. They are called the minimas and are the hardest workers of all. They take the new pieces of leaves and clean them. Then they cut them into smaller pieces and chew them into fine pellets

THE MONKEY-FACED
Orchid

DECLARE HIS GLORY . . .

his wonders

among all people.

PSALM 96:3

THE MONKEY-FACED
Orchid

Many years ago in Costa Rica I was out on an orchid hunt with some friends. The jungle was at its best. The trees were wet and very green right after a drenching rain. We found an orchid plant that I had never seen before. My native guide got excited. "This," he announced triumphantly as he showed us the succulent plant, "is an *orquídea cara de mono,* or monkey-faced orchid, *Dressleria dilecta.*"

Since my friend already had this orchid in his collec-

Papayo Mountain, the host of the monkey-faced orchid.

tion, he gave me the plant. I took it home to adorn my ever-growing orchid garden. First I chose a chunk of root from a giant fern. These ferns produce a big porous root mass that makes excellent material to grow orchids on. Though many people think orchids are parasites that draw their nutrition from the plants they attach themselves to, they only use their hosts for anchoring their roots. They live on the air, water, and debris that collect on their roots.

I tenderly placed the plant on the fern root and wrapped the orchid's roots around it. Then I tied the orchid onto the fern root with thin strips of inner tube to hold the plant in place till its roots caught on. Last I hooked a wire into the fern root and hung it in my collection under a tree with the perfect amount of shade. When the plant bloomed, I would carry it into my office so the whole family could enjoy the blooms.

Sure enough, that first rainy season it got ready to bloom. The buds were so unique and round. I watched them every day.

Finally the buds burst open and I admired the whitish, fragrant flowers. Right away I noticed the odd shape of the flower and grinned at the thought of its unique name. I had never seen a monkey face in the flower, but I still always called it the monkey-faced orchid. *It must just be because of its funny shape,* I mused. *Monkey-faced orchid . . .*

When we moved to Waslala, Nicaragua, I left my precious orchid collection behind in Costa Rica. Thirteen years passed, and I had almost forgotten about the monkey-faced orchid. But then Kevin Steiner (a friend from Managua), my son Kenny, and I were exploring the renowned Papayo Mountain

The monkey-faced orchid's buds.

that looms over Waslala. We had almost reached the mountain's crown and were having so much fun.

Everything was wet from the frequent showers during the rainy season. Thick wads of the greenest moss hung from every branch. Colorful birds sang in the treetops. Butterflies with azure blue wings floated past. The wind was moist and fog laden and blessed us with its many cool caresses. I watched the trail, of course; if not, I might have fallen in the mud. But I also watched the trees for orchids. Then I saw it. Right in plain sight, about twenty feet above the ground. My memory stick blinked and kicked into orchid mode.

"Boys," I shouted, pointing above me, "I see something very special up in that tree.

"Pablo, I hope it was worth the climb!"

I think it's a monkey-faced orchid, and it has buds!"

After much debate on how to get the plant down, Kevin offered his skills. He shinnied up a sapling next to the thicker tree, worked his way over, and then clung to the bigger tree with all the strength of his one arm. With the other hand he ripped off the handsome plant.

"Careful," I warned. "Try not to break off the buds."

Kevin inched his way back down the tree. Suddenly his arm gave out. *Swoosh!* He scooted down that tree a lot faster than he had gone up and landed at the foot of the tree, where he of course stopped abruptly. He got up and with a big grin held the plant out to me. Safe and sound!

"Thanks so much, Kevin!"

On the way home I walked very carefully. The trail was muddy and slick. I held my precious monkey-faced orchid in one hand, protecting it and its buds. With the other hand I carried a sack of less exotic orchids to add to my collection. The trail was very steep at places. Kenny and I were laughing at Kevin because he fell so often in his treadless crocs. We started counting how many times he fell. When the count reached five, we laughed harder. I was last on the trail now, proud as a peacock because I hadn't fallen once. Of course, I was wearing a pair of boots with good tread, and I was used to the Waslala hills. I shouldn't be falling! Then we came to a very steep place. I dug in my heels like an expert. Kevin fell flat on his back again—his sixth time. Kevin and Kenny had just gone around a bend in the trail, and I was almost at the foot of the steep place. I was sure I was out of the danger zone. Great!

Then it happened. I still don't know how. *Whamo!* I fell flat on my side in the mud. I didn't reach out my hands to break my fall because I was protecting my precious orchids. So my poor old ribs took the beating. My breath suddenly seemed far, far away, and a very sharp pain sneaked into my chest. I knew I couldn't get up for a little while. So I lay on the trail and laughed. Hey, it sure beat crying! When they came back and found me lying there

> **"Euni was staring at the strange flowers. Suddenly she announced, "I see the monkey face!""**

in the mud, they laughed too. But at least my precious monkey-faced orchid was safe and sound!

After about a week, my new orchid bloomed. I was so happy. Sure enough,

the flower had a weird shape. But though it looked hilarious, I still didn't see a monkey face. Soon I was carrying it around and showing it to everybody, excited about my new orchid. Most everyone just shrugged. *Yeah, just Pablo making a pest out of himself. We've seen his orchids before. He's always sticking them under our noses.*

But my dear wife Euni actually took time to listen and look. "See, they're called monkey-faced orchids," I explained. "I don't know why. But they sure are neat, and they smell good."

Euni was staring at the strange flowers. Suddenly she announced, "I see the monkey face!"

"Where?" I almost shouted, trying to see what she saw.

"You have to line it up just right, honey," Euni continued. "See, there's the hole in the flower that's shaped like a monkey's face. But you can't see the eyes—those red dots in the heart of the flower—until they line up just right. Like this . . ."

Then I saw it and burst out laughing. The outside of the flower was shaped like a monkey's head. In the center, the flower had a hole that created the exact shape for the face; and now, right out of the heart of the flower, two beady, impish eyes peered out at me. A mischievous little monkey! Now I laughed again because he was sticking his tongue out at me. I had found my monkey at last. And to think that my dear wife beat me to it!

What do you think God was thinking when He made this orchid? Imagine Him planning just how He would make it. I'm not sure what He was thinking, but I believe He was grinning. Monkeys,

You have to line it up just right.

and comical orchids that look like them, show us that God has a unique sense of humor. He created us humans with the ability to laugh. Animals can't laugh. He made us so we could laugh; then He gave us plenty of things to laugh about. So today I want you to appreciate God and His humor. And have yourself a good laugh as you look at this comical monkey. Enjoy it and let it make your day!

Monkeys, and comical orchids
that look like them, show us that God has a unique sense of humor.

The Blind, Headless, Tailless Creature

AND GOD MADE . . .

every thing that creepeth

. . . and God saw that it was good.

Genesis 1:25

THE BLIND, HEADLESS, *Tailless Creature*

One day I was cleaning out a ditch behind the house. My children were watching. I was picking up an old, broken cement block when under it we saw a strange creature wriggling around, desperately trying to find a hole to crawl into to get away from our prying eyes. "Is it a snake?" Kenny cried.

"Nope."

"Daddy, what is that thing?"

"Is it an earthworm?" Cynthia asked.

"Nope. It actually eats earthworms."

"Is it an eel?" Luana inquired.

"Nope. It sure looks like one, and that's what I used to call it, 'the blind eel,' but now I know it's not an eel."

"Is it a lizard without feet?"

"Nope. It doesn't have feet, that's for sure, but it's not a lizard. Its closest relative might be the salamander."

I reached down and grabbed the gray, snake-like creature that I knew would not bite me. It was very hard to hold because some slimy goop seeped out of its skin and made my hand all smeary and yucky. Gripping it tightly in my fist, I held it up for the children to get a look. "This creature is called a caecilian (sih SIHL yuhn), *Gymnopis multiplicata*. It's a long, headless, limbless, burrowing amphibian."

"What's an amphibian?" Kenny wondered.

"An amphibian is an animal that begins its life in the water and later emerges to live on land. It's the family of frogs, toads, and salamanders. The caecilian is an amphibian. That's why you were all wrong when you guessed it was a snake, a worm, an eel, or a lizard."

I brought the two ends of the caecilian together. "Look, children. Can you see from where you stand which is the back and which is the front?"

"No," Cynthia chuckled. "Does it even have a head or a tail?"

"Come, look closely. See its underdeveloped eyes? They are so tiny and are closed completely. They are blind. These critters live under leaves and sticks, under rocks and logs, and underground. They don't need to see. They only come out into the open when it rains hard. During the rain they sneak out and catch earthworms escaping to the surface from their waterlogged tunnels. They track them down by their smell.

"Underground, they forage for creatures like worms, termites, and little larvae. Get me a knife, Cynthia; I want to show you its teeth.

"See its tiny nose holes? It breathes out of its nose, but it doesn't use it to smell like we do. It smells with these tiny tentacles right beside its eyes."

"Daddy, how do they dig their tunnels without feet?"

"Watch. These little guys are great diggers." I turned the little creature loose in

If you look closely, you can see its underdeveloped eyes.

the ditch again. Just like a snake, it began wriggling and working its head into the dirt and leaves in the ditch. Soon it disappeared into the soft dirt under the debris.

"Children, you should have held the caecilian and felt how strong its muscles are. It's actually hard to hold one. Plus, the bones in its body are made in a special compact way that can take the hard pushing. It has a tough, rubbery nose shaped a little like a spade. It just slams that old spade into the dirt and wiggles it back and forth and up and down, and the soil just gets out of the way. 'Here I come, the mighty caecilian!' They are excellent diggers."

I held out my hands. "You'd better be glad you didn't hold the caecilian. See how yucky my hands are? He puts out a goop that is toxic to some animals. But it is not poisonous for the coral snake. They love to grab and swallow caecilians. Several other snakes eat caecilians, and some birds will pick them up if they happen to see them above ground. But most animals are smarter than I and just let them go. Let me go wash my hands!"

As I rinsed them off in the creek, I asked, "Children, did you know that we could have a lot of caecilians here on our place?"

"No. We never see them!"

"That's because they spend most of their time underground. We might be walking over one right now, just like we walk over earthworms all the time. But God made it so they are hardly seen at all. That's the way He protects them. Isn't it neat how God takes care of all the animals? Every animal has a unique, God-given setup just for it."

"And he made us the same way," Luana interjected. "We know how to do what we are made to do. I can't dig underground with my nose like a caecilian, but I can sure wash dishes!"

"That's right. God made everything special, and it's all for us to enjoy and for His glory and honor. Even the caecilian."

This fellow's nose is also his shovel.

The White Tent-Making

bats

CANST THOU BY SEARCHING
find out God?

JOB 11:7

Chapter 9

THE WHITE TENT-MAKING bats

La Tirimbina. The name sounded strangely familiar to me. My friend was just telling me that he had been there and had been enchanted by the trails through the rain forest. Years ago, when I was growing up in Costa Rica, I had heard about La Tirimbina. We spoke of it as a place so far back in that you'd get lost just thinking about it. Now my friend was saying he had been there.

But what my friend said next really made my ears tingle. "They showed us the white bats."

"They what?" I almost shouted. "They showed you the white bats? You can't be serious!"

I had been reading about tiny, white bats that lived in tents, just like Abraham, Isaac, and Jacob. Now I was actually talking to someone who had seen them! "Where?"

"La Tirimbina, of course!"

Several days later my son swung our green Isuzu Trooper off the highway that leads to Puerto Viejo de Sarapiquí,

Taken by Jacinto Yoder at
La Tirimbina Biological
Reserve, Costa Rica

Seven little white tent bats hanging upside down in their neat little tent.

Costa Rica, and into a driveway half hidden by heliconias and bougainvilleas. Nope, I didn't miss the sign: "Reserva Biológica La Tirimbina" (La Tirimbina Biological Reserve).

We parked the Trooper in a lovely area that was really a tropical park. Soon we sat

This brown tent bat lives in a safe haven he built himself.

in Bernal Rodríguez's office hearing all about La Tirimbina. We were especially impressed that the money the many tourists, including us, paid to come to La Tirimbina didn't go into somebody's bottomless pocket, but was used to educate the local people about nature. While we were there, we saw groups of school children receiving all kinds of teaching on the natural things that abound in La Tirimbina.

But best of all, Bernal and I talked about bats. For the next forty minutes we really got batty. I discovered that he specialized in tent bats. He had even written several books on bats and one on tent bats in particular. We left La Tirimbina in a downpour, but our hearts were full of anticipation. Our bat fever was running dangerously high, and we had an appointment with the bats the next morning at eight.

The next morning found my son Jacinto, a guide named Daniel, and me on the jungle trail looking for bats. We crossed the longest hanging footbridge in Central America. We saw the broad-billed motmot. We surprised a porcupine sleeping in a low tree. We found a string of huge ants. The guide almost fainted when I held them in my hand. He warned me of what I already knew—that their awful sting can actually make you sick! But I'll tell you more about them in the next chapter.

We viewed orchids, birds, butterflies, trees, mushrooms, caimans, and so much more. A walk deep into the rain forest is an adventure any day!

Taken by Jacinto Yoder at La Tirimbina Biological Reserve, Costa Rica

Taken by Jacinto Yoder at La Tirimbina Biological Reserve, Costa Rica

Taken by Jacinto Yoder at La Tirimbina Biological Reserve, Costa Rica

We weren't on the trail long until Daniel was pointing out the bat tents. There are about twenty-two different kinds of tent bats identified in Bernal's book *Neotropical Tent-Roosting Bats.* As we walked along, Daniel explained how a bat hangs under different leaves and chews certain parts of the leaf until it breaks. Once broken, the leaf parts that hang down create a

> **"Daniel approached the leaf noiselessly, bent over, and peeped under its edge. The big smile on his face told me the whole story."**

perfect tent for the bat to use as a roost.

But invariably, as we hiked along the trail, our conversation floated back to the white tent-making bats. "Are you sure we can see them today?" I asked.

"Well, I can't promise," Daniel replied. "But we did see them yesterday. I can't let you go back to the same tent, because they spook easily and if we visit too frequently we'll scare them away. But there are three areas where we often find them. Just wait and see."

Daniel continued explaining that Caribbean white tent bats, *Ectophylla alba,* are rare. I guessed he was right, because in all my forty years of traipsing through jungles, I had never seen a white bat. But now just maybe I would. (They are only found in Honduras, Nicaragua, Costa Rica, and Panama along the Caribbean side of the continental divide.)

The white bat only uses heliconia leaves for its tent. Heliconia leaves are very much like banana leaves, only smaller. So now I was watching the heliconias along the trail like a hawk.

We were two hours into our adventure and still hadn't seen a white bat when Daniel suggested, "Let's try the island."

The Sarapiquí River is one of the most beautiful, clear rivers I have ever seen. The water sparkles blue as it gushes over the tons of rock spread along its bottom. In La Tirimbina the river has a several-acre island that few people ever invade. We took the overgrown trail that runs all the way around the island. After half an hour on the trail, stopping at every heliconia patch, I suddenly noticed a heliconia leaf stretched out over the trail about chest high. It hung broadside, so it was difficult for me to tell if it had been chewed and broken or not. But just in case, I hissed, "Hey, quiet, there might be some bats under that leaf."

Daniel approached the leaf noiselessly, bent over, and peeped under its edge. The big smile on his face told me the whole story. I could see he was excited. Then he warned us, "Look, let's be very careful not to scare them away. If we do, they may never come back, and it takes them over a week to make a new tent. Every couple of months they have to make a new one,

Taken by Jacinto Yoder at La Tirimbina
Biological Reserve, Costa Rica

Finally up ahead we glimpsed the white tent bat's abode, sticking out over our trail.

because the old leaf rots. But let's not be the cause today, okay?"

Jacinto swung into full action now. He got his camera ready and took some sample shots of other leaves close by. I held my eager naturalist passion in check and waited for my turn to peep at the bats until the photos were taken. I knew that if they flew while Jacinto took the photos, I might never get my chance to see the cute little critters cuddled up so cozily in their tent.

"You may take three shots with flash," Daniel suggested as Jacinto eased himself onto the forest floor. Right by the trail ran a leaf cutter ant highway. Jacinto lay flat on his back, just on the edge of their trail. He held perfectly still, and I could see that he was doing his best. He and the camera just merged and worked like a team. Slowly his hand adjusted the focus. *Pop!*

The flash did not chase away the bats. Later Jacinto told me the bats had their little heads tucked up into their own fuzzy bodies. After the first flash, several peeped a little, enabling him to get a photo of their faces. We asked Daniel for permission to take one extra photo, and soon Jacinto had four photos stored away on the memory card. He then crawled away, knocking off ants as he stood up.

Tiny balls of cott
. . . oops! I mea
white tent bats

Taken by Jacinto Yoder at La Tirimbi
Biological Reserve, Costa Rica

Then it was my turn. I eased myself down on my back and scooted over noiselessly until I was right beside the ants and straight under the tent. I was almost holding my breath. What I saw still warms my heart today. Seven tiny balls of what looked like cotton. The little creatures looked so fragile and white! And so cuddly!

The tiny little bats were so timid. They didn't want to look at me. But I did get a glimpse of their faces as they partially peeped out.

Daniel then told us how Bernal had actually watched the little tykes make their tents. They choose a leaf that is still sticking up toward the sky. By the time the week is up, and from the weight of the seven little bats, the leaf hangs parallel to the ground, just perfect for their tent. They split the nighttime between feeding on fruit and tent making. They crawl upside down along the heliconia leaf's midrib and chew along the main stem on both sides. After chewing so far, the bat pulls the leaf

downward with his claws. Then the leaf topples and makes a perfect tent.

Now it was time to say goodbye. I took it all in for the last time. The seven little bats didn't mind at all that I was watching them. They looked so cozy and protected hanging there. No wind or rain could get them. No opossum would be likely to find

I could see the little tyke's face as he peeped out at me.

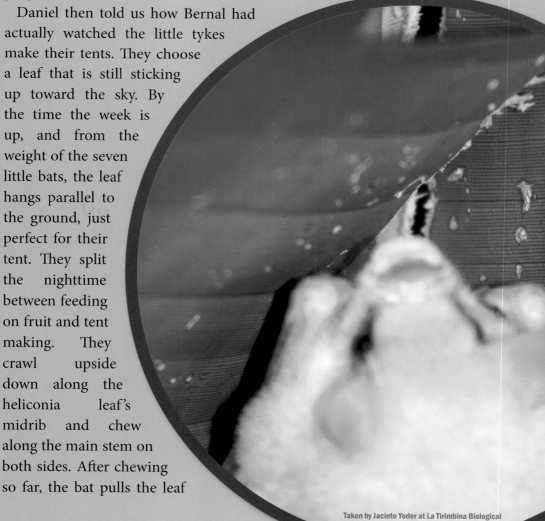

Taken by Jacinto Yoder at La Tirimbina Biological Reserve, Costa Rica

them. I again realized that I was looking at one of God's very, very special creatures. Not only had He done a wonderful job in planning and creating this cute little bat, but He was also giving me a rare opportunity of seeing it in the wild.

I edged away from my comrades, the leaf cutter ants. I got up and brushed the debris from my shoulders. We packed our gear and left silently, almost reverently. The bats were not disturbed. We were all happy. And in a very real way, seeing the white bat with its special design, engineering abilities, and super hideout brought glory and honor to the Creator. Especially in my heart!

See their teeth marks?

Taken by Jacinto Yoder at La Tirimbina Biological Reserve, Costa Rica

THE MEANEST STING
in the Jungle

REMEMBER HIS
marvellous works
that he hath done .

1 CHRONICLES 16:12

Chapter 10

THE MEANEST STING
in the Jungle

The jungle was steaming hot. We were literally dripping with sweat as we clambered down the mountainside. The green canopy that engulfed us and had felt so cool in the morning now embraced the heat of the sun and pressed it down on us. But it didn't matter; in another fifteen minutes we would be off the mountain and, after a short walk, we'd be swimming in the cool, green waters of the Río Toro (Bull River). This was San Carlos, Costa Rica, at its best!

Early that morning we had set out to explore Cerro Blanco (White Mountain). Several of my brothers, some friends, and Philip Stoltzfus, my brother-in-law fresh from the States, made up our crew. We had hiked to the top of the mountain first and then hung our heads right over the edge of the cliff that towered there, showing off its grand four to five hundred feet of sheer rock.

After experiencing the peak, we descended halfway down the other side of the mountain and approached the cliff at its middle. We were shooting for the cave, a hole right in the middle of the cliff, a neat navel for the white rock's belly. Fortunately, the jungle wrapped around close to the cave on the left side. All we had to do was cross a narrow rock ledge and we were safely in

Majestic Cerro Blanco

© Duane Nisly

the cave. Once there, we were hanging high above the river bottom, under half of the mountain, and yet on top of the world.

I have always loved to explore this shallow cave. You never know what you'll find next. The first time we explored it many years ago, we found a fine pair of owlets. Once we camped in the dry cave, and our campfire spooked the people who passed on the road below. A few times we found the legendary, soft, dangling nests of the lesser swallow-tailed swift. Today we had seen the rare king vulture showing off his bright colors as he soared above us against the indigo blue sky.

Now we were on our way off the mountain, tired, but happy. There was no bone ache or weariness that the sulfurous waters of the Río Toro couldn't cure!

Several times during the day I had warned Philip, "Watch before you grab." That slogan is very important for any jun-

> **"You are bound to get your fist full of thorns, or get stung by some spiny caterpillar, or get bitten by the wicked eyelash viper."**

gle hiker. If you blindly grab at any branch or tree or vine as you climb, you are bound to get your fist full of thorns, or get stung by some spiny caterpillar, or even get bitten by the wicked eyelash viper that hangs around in the bushes and low trees. Philip knew the rules.

We approached a fallen tree that had slashed open a small clearing in the jungle when it fell. These open spaces are special little windows in the thick jungle that let the sun penetrate the dark wetness. Often these open spaces attract butterflies, other insects, and the birds that eat them. Today I was in too much of a hurry to explore. I just wiped the sweat off my face with my handkerchief one more time, took my machete, and began to whack my way through the brush. I had to jump over the branches of the fallen tree. They were bleached with age and very dry in the sunlight. Right in the center of the brush I hit them. Bees!

Fortunately, the bees were not the kind that sting and make you howl, but they were the sticky kind that fly into your hair and pester you with their incessant buzzing and their tiny, harmless pinches. Soon I was swatting them away from my hair and hollering, "Boys, I hit bees! These bees don't actually sting; but they get into your hair and clothes and drive you crazy!"

I looked back at Philip. He tried to look brave, but I could see he was uneasy at the thought of plowing into a brush pile infested with bees, harmless though they might be. But he followed bravely, swatting at the ornery critters as he jumped over the fallen branches. Then it happened. He reached out and grabbed one of the white, dry branches that lay horizontally along the trail. He jerked his hand back and howled, "Ouch!"

I had stopped just beyond the brush pile to wait on my comrades, so I saw it

next moment he was using both hands to swat the pesky bees. All the while he was groaning and moaning. And I knew why.

The black creature that had been scampering along the dry, white branch was no joke. It was the famous *Paraponera clavata*, the awful bullet ant. I had been stung too, once upon a time, and I knew that Philip's hand felt as if a bullet had literally been shot into it, thus the mean name. Trying to hide my laughter, I ushered Philip down off the mountain and into the sulfurous waters of the Río Toro, hoping the cool water and its

This giant tropical ant measures an inch long.

Taken by Jacinto Yoder at La Tirimbina Biological Reserve, Costa Rica

all. And, to my shame, I laughed. Hard. Philip was coming through the brush now, high stepping like a thoroughbred, desperate to reach the safety of the jungle's embrace. One moment his left hand clutched his stung right hand, and the

minerals would ease the awful pain.

These large ants build their nests at the base of jungle trees. They dig various tunnels that go down a foot deep and then branch out into different chambers and compartments. A healthy nest might have 1,000 to 1,500 ants. During the day and night, the worker ants leave their homes to forage for food. They forage

Taken by Jacinto Yoder at La Tirimbina
Biological Reserve, Costa Rica

This worker is taking home his dinner—a bee.

all the way from the forest floor to the highest jungle canopy. They bring in arthropods, other invertebrates, and small insects they find dead. If the insects are alive, they attack and kill them with their awful sting. They also bring in nectar and water for their young.

When a nest is disturbed, a dozen of these deadly creatures swarm out to attack. They also give out a musty, stinky smell to warn everybody to get back. They squeak and click their awful mandibles. While foraging, they are not very aggressive, though they will sting if threatened (as when Phil-

ip laid his hand right on one).

When my son Jacinto and I had walked the trails at La Tirimbina Biological Reserve in Costa Rica, I had noticed a small tree that had bullet ants running up and down its trunk. Sure enough, they had a nest at the tree's base. We stopped to get some photos. After taking the photos for this chapter, I suggested we take a photo of an ant on someone's hand. Our guide looked at me as if I had lost my mind.

"On your hand? Not on mine!"

"Listen," I explained, "you have to show it on a hand so you can compare the size with something. If you only see it on a leaf, you will never know how big the ant really is."

"Neither do you know how painful the sting is," he assured me, "or you wouldn't be acting so crazy!"

I studied the tree carefully. I watched the ants come in, some with their mouths full and others apparently empty, though I guessed they carried nectar in their mandibles.

They had a road they all used. At one point their highway left the tree trunk and followed a small sapling down toward home. Here, I knew, was my chance. I waited until there were no ants on the sapling for the moment. Then I grabbed the sapling in my fist, down low. I waited until an ant trotted down the sapling toward my hand. I closed my other fist

> ## I closed my fist around the sapling above the ant. He looked big and menacing . . .

around the sapling above the ant. He looked big and menacing, and the guide hollered, "Don't you dare! Don't you realize how those creatures hurt when they sting you? They can actually give you a fever and make you sick!"

"Yeah, I know," I answered calmly. Grinning at him, I continued, "I have no intention of asking him to sting me. I just need a photo of him on my hand."

The guide gave up, shaking his head in disbelief. The trapped ant did not want to crawl onto my hand. He ran back and forth from fist to fist, trying to escape. But he was well trapped. Then, just as I expected, he very timidly crawled up onto my hand. I slowly lifted my hand away from the branch; then, holding it out to Jacinto, I hissed, "Jacinto, take a photo, quick!"

Jacinto snapped a couple of photos, and in very short order I had my fist back on the sapling and the ant was scampering home.

Why was the guide so concerned that the ant would sting me? Why did big, forty-year-old Philip Stoltzfus cry out when he grabbed the ant by mistake? Why do people say that the bullet ant's sting is the most painful sting in the jungle? Let me explain.

Justin O. Schmidt is an entomologist who has been stung by hundreds of insects. Studying creepy, crawly creatures is his job. He designed a scale to tell how much a sting hurts. The scale is actually called the Justin O. Schmidt Pain Index. His pain scale runs from one to four, with higher numbers for greater pain. A regular bee sting is categorized as one on his scale. The awful Africanized "killer" bee sting is categorized at two. The only insect that really registers four on this scale is . . . you guessed it, the bullet ant.

Upstream from the breach the water was crystal clear. Downstream the water was blue. The breach in between was what interested me.

was coming from ran lengthwise with the creek at a slight angle. It sure enough looked as if there were a log under the water where the river made its change. But what really surprised me was that the breach that produced the bluing was not blue at all, but white. It shone out from under the water with a resplendent glow.

I took the photos I needed; then I did what I had been itching to do ever since I had gotten there. I jumped in. The water was very cold, just like all Costa Rican streams are at that high altitude. I waded up to the breach carefully. Would the water be hot? Would there be some blast of sulfur that would burn us? No, it was just this twenty-five-foot-long white breach on the creek bottom that somehow made the water blue.

And there was a log, and the bluing was coming out from under the log.

As we straddled the breach in waist-deep water, we felt the warmth. The bluing that seeped out of the breach was volcano hot. The hot water soon mixed with the cold water, and by the time it got to our legs, it only made the water nice and warm.

I had the nerve to reach down into the breach. The closer I got to the gap in the sand, the hotter it got. And all along the gap, where the heat seeped out, everything was a blazing white. Was it the heat that made it white? After the white area where the heat seeped out, everything was stained with the same blue as the water. My friend and I soon pulled out a piece of log that was stained blue. Once out of the water, it lost some of its richness, yet you could see the blue on the rough, wet wood.

I grew up beside the Río Toro (Bull River) in Pital de San Carlos, Costa Rica. That river had a high sulfur content. Sometimes the water was greenish. Sometimes it got really strong and milky white. When the water lay still, it became brackish, with a tint of rust and red. But always the water smelled of sulfur and was bitter to the taste. People claimed that the cattle that drank the sulfurous water were the healthiest in the area. We always claimed that we were healthier because we swam in it almost daily. There was no question why the Río Toro water was different. It was sulfur saturated!

Now, up to my waist in warm, blue water, I wondered. This blue water did not stink. It did not taste bad. It just did not resemble sulfur at all. And yet the warmth made it clear that it was volcanic. Blue Creek was sky blue. It must be, I concluded, that volcanoes don't only produce hot sulfur. They also produce a blue something that makes the water so lovely.

We hiked down off the mountain, tired, but with nature happy hearts. I had seen something totally new in nature that blessed me. No, I still hadn't figured out what the bluing was, but I knew who set up the whole system.

After researching the cause of the bluing, I found out that scientists don't really know why the water turns blue. Upstream there is a fork in the creek, and they believe it could partly be a mixture of chemicals, perhaps sulfur and calcium carbonate, from those two creeks. But though the tourists and scientists who go there are baffled, I believe that four thousand years ago, when the fountains of the great deep were broken up, there were some areas where lovely blue water spewed out with the rest. And today, many years later, such a stream still exists to give evidence of our Creator God.

The breach that produced the bluing was not blue at all. It was a resplendent white that shone right through the crystal-clear water.

THE BUG WITH
the Big Nose

AND GOD SAW EVERY THING
that he had made,
and, behold, it was very good.

GENESIS 1:31

Chapter 12

THE BUG WITH
the Big Nose

My daughter's scream was blood-curdling. And yet she was standing in our living room in broad daylight. No reason in the world that she should be scared.

"Come on, Cynthia, try again. I promise . . ." (That's something I need to do at times so my children believe me, trickster that I am.) ". . . that old bug is as harmless as a kitty. Just reach down and pick him up," I commanded with a flourish.

"I'm not scared of a bug," my next-older daughter, Luana, bragged. "I'll pick him up."

Luana marched right over to the bug on the living room floor and bent over to pick him up. Then the bug did it again! And Luana's scream was just as loud as Cynthia's. And just as authentic. And I confess that even I jumped.

· · · · · · · · · · · · · · · · · ·

The perfect camouflage.

· · · · · · · · · · · · · · · · · ·

What was going on that made my daughters scream?

My dear friend Julio had called me on the radio the evening before and told me that a very strange bug had just flown into the light of his house. He declared that he hadn't seen anything like it be-

The only bug I know that has its eyes almost at its waist.

fore and described its eyes as set way back, almost to its waist, behind a nose as big as a peanut. My naturalist blood started pumping faster. "A *machaca!*" I yelled over the radio.

But Julio had no idea what a *machaca* was.

I had never seen a *machaca (Fulgora laternaria)* in Nicaragua before, though I had seen many of them in Costa Rica, where the climate was similar. But now I was having one sent to me. I opened the little box carefully. As the lid popped open and the big bug walked out in such a stately manner, I yelled too. But it was out of joy, not fear.

Now here was the *machaca* perched on the floor of my living room, and my daughters couldn't even pick him up. And I was still laughing hard. I knew what was happening, but they didn't.

I tried again. "The *machaca* is perfectly harmless."

"But Daddy, he jumps and makes such a funny noise, I couldn't help but scream. And you knew it all along!" Cynthia rebuked me.

The peanut-head bug really is a harmless homopteran, closely related to the cicada. The homoptera group also includes aphids, whiteflies, and other insects that have forewings of uniform texture. In every Latin American country where this bug lives, a legend runs freely about the terrible *machaca* and its deadly bite. When I was a young fellow in Costa Rica, I had learned a wild song about this bug and its bite. I had always wondered if the bug really was dangerous.

The peanut-head bug does not bite, nor sting, nor do anything else that's painful. But the peanut-head bug can give you a fright!

Like many other insects, these bugs

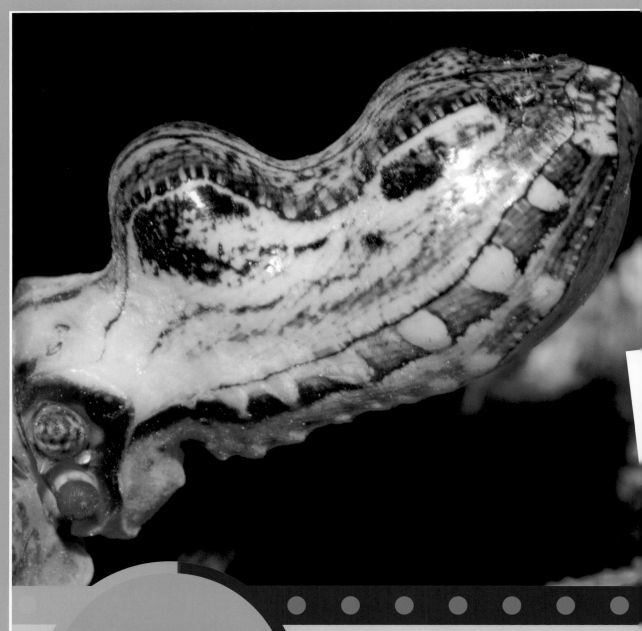

This bug's fantastic nose is hollow and extremely light. He uses it as a drum to scare away his enemies.

were made with incredible camouflage. They spend most of their time crawling around on the trunks of guapinol trees. Their dappled gray and brown color matches the tree's bark perfectly. Most people walk right past a guapinol tree and never see a thing. But since the bugs make a tasty meal for some smart capuchin monkey or flying brown jay, they have an extra trick to protect themselves. Just ask Luana or Cynthia.

When the capuchin monkey or the jay or my daughters come too close, the bug becomes very dramatic. First he is holding perfectly still, wings tucked in, big nose resting against the tree bark—a perfect picture of peace and quiet. But when anything gets too close, something snaps. It's like the bug is wound up tightly with some sort of a spring. When danger comes, it pulls the trigger!

Here he is after he snapped, wings spread open. What does he look like? An alligator? A dinosaur? A monster?

When the peanut-head bug comes alive, it all happens at once. In a terrific whir, his wings pop open, he vibrates his head against the bark (or living room floor), and he lets out a gust of brown, stinky dust. It happens so abruptly that it even made me jump, and I was five yards away.

> ## It happens so abruptly that it even made me jump, and I was five yards away.

It made Luana scream. It almost made Cynthia faint!

Now imagine a high-strung capuchin monkey. His sharp eyes see a peanut-head bug clinging to a guapinol trunk. First the bug scoots around the back of the tree to avoid the monkey's slippery fingers. But the monkey follows. Just as the monkey's paw descends, the bug explodes. Not only does the drumming of his nose against the tree trunk and the sudden whir of wings scare the monkey, nor just the puff of stinky dust, but when the bug pops open his wings, he takes on a very peculiar shape. He grows to double his size in a flash. A large set of angry eyes painted onto his wings stare at you. The big nose and all the rest of his attire make him look like a miniature alligator or some dangerous dinosaur. I can imagine the monkey staring at the bug for a split second and then running through the treetops as fast as he can go.

I confess that this morning I'm glad I'm not some brown jay wanting to dine on peanut-head bug. It would be the most frightening lunch I'd ever tasted! I'll stick with my rice and beans; wouldn't you?

When I think of something very special as I write this, I shake my head about as fast as the *machaca*. Evolution could never come up with something as exciting as the peanut-head bug. But I am sure our God could. I can just imagine Him when He said the word, and the peanut-head bugs started to fly around that first guapinol tree. He probably smiled and said, "It is good!"

The Daddy That Carries His Baby on His Back

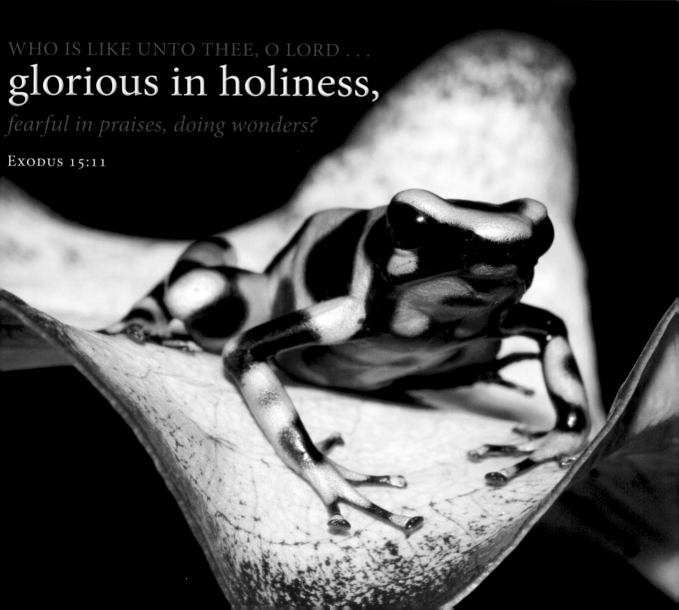

WHO IS LIKE UNTO THEE, O LORD . . .

glorious in holiness,

fearful in praises, doing wonders?

Exodus 15:11

THE DADDY THAT CARRIES
His Baby on His Back

Many years ago I took three children on a nature walk. With their mama's permission, we headed for the jungle not more than a fifteen-minute walk from their house. Our destination was a creek deep in the jungle's interior.

Yesenia, Lucrecia, and Hector were used to the jungle since they lived so close to it. Their mother, Mary Jane, had instilled the love of nature in them. Now we held a lively conversation as we traipsed through the grassy fields.

"We had a horde of army ants attack us one night," ten-year-old Yesenia told me. "That was quite an experience!"

"It sure was," seven-year-old Lucrecia added. "Thousands of ants crawled over everything. We woke up when they started to bite us, and we had to leave the house and wait outside until they were done."

"They cleaned up the house! They ate all the roaches, the spiders, and even the scorpions!" Yesenia explained.

"Wow! Weren't you afraid?" I asked, looking at little five-year-old Hector.

"Nah, I wasn't scared. My daddy told me we just had to wait until they left."

"How long were you outside in the dark waiting on the ants to clean your house?" I asked Yesenia.

"I don't know. Maybe an hour and a half. But it seemed longer than that!"

"What do you think we will find in the woods today?" I asked.

"Maybe we'll find a snake," Lucrecia giggled. "I won't even be scared of it."

That's the way our excursion started that day. A lively day with a lively bunch.

We hiked down to the creek and had our swim. We admired the many interesting things that the jungle had to offer us that day. On the way home we found the creature that took the cake.

"Look!" Hector hollered, pointing to the leaf-covered forest floor. "There's a frog!"

We were all excited right away. The loveliest green and black frog hopped away from us as fast as he could. As he hopped along, I told the children the little frog's story. "This is a poison dart frog. There are many kinds of them in the world. This one is very attractive because of his lovely

A handsome
ntleman perched
on a tropical
eliconia flower.

color design. Isn't he darling?"

"Yes, he is terribly cute, but why are they called poison dart frogs?" Yesenia wondered.

"These frogs are called poison dart frogs because some species have a very potent poison under their skin. The Indians used these frogs to poison their darts. They would pierce them with a sharp stick and hold them over a fire. The poison would secrete from their skin, and the Indians would rub their darts in it.

"The Indians used the darts in their blowguns, which consisted of long, hollow, pipe-like pieces of thin bamboo. They would stick a dart into the pipe, aim it toward their prey, and blow fast and hard. The dart would fly out and pierce the victim's skin. The poison would attack the nervous system and paralyze the ani-

> **The Indians would stick a dart into the pipe, aim it toward their prey, and blow fast and hard.**

mal. But the meat was still good to eat if cooked."

"How does a blowgun work?" Lucrecia asked.

"We used a blowgun when I was a teenager. We made them out of my mother's aluminum curtain rods. Chico, a Costa Rican, showed me how to make little mud balls and blow them at birds. You make little balls that fit tightly in the pipe. Next you spit on the little balls until they are as slick as soap. Then you place one into the end of the pipe, hold it to your mouth, and *splat!*

"Chico was such a good shot that he could often bring a bird down. The mud ball would usually only stun the birds, and we would keep them as pets. Those were the days when all of our cages were running over with red-legged honeycreepers, yellow-crowned euphonias, and golden-hooded tanagers. We got good at shooting blowguns too, but never as good as Chico. His best show was when he went automatic. He'd make half a dozen perfect mud balls, pop them all into his mouth, and then he had a six-shooter, high-powered and automatic. Those six balls zipped into the treetops faster than you could count them. Then his spit was as red as clay for a good while."

The children laughed as they pictured the short, stocky Costa Rican spitting clay.

"By far the worst thing we discovered was how fun it was to shoot at each other. I don't think the Indians did that. At least not to their friends. The poisoned darts killed. They used them to bring down birds, monkeys, squirrels, and even peccaries and tapirs."

I peered more closely at our small friend. "Look!" I exclaimed. "This frog has a tiny tadpole on his back. He is taking it to its own little waterhole. But wait; let me tell you the whole story.

"The *Dendrobates auratus* mostly lives

© Martin Shields/photographerdirect.com

This frog is a really good father. He carries the baby.

on the jungle floor. When the rainy season starts around the middle of May, it becomes very active. The rains announce mating season. The female finds a moist, cool place and lays five or six eggs, usually among the dead leaves on the jungle floor. Once the eggs hatch, the daddy frog hops over and straddles the nest. With most varieties of poison dart frogs, Mama does this job, but in this species, Daddy carries the babies. One little tadpole climbs up on his

back and hangs on tight. Then Daddy goes to find a place for his little taddy to live."

"Where do they take them?" Lucrecia wondered.

"They find small pools of water wherever they can—knotholes in trees, bromeliad cups that are always full of water in the rainy season, or rocks that have hollows in them that fill up with rainwater. They even place their babies in old tin cans and abandoned plates and bowls. After finding a place for each baby, Daddy Frog backs into the water and the taddy swims free. The tadpoles eat algae and little dead creatures they find in the water."

"How long does it take until they drop their tails and hop away?" Yesenia asked.

"Around two months."

And that's the way our adventure ended that day. We arrived back at their cabin in high spirits. They were soon telling their nature-loving mother all about the things we had seen. By far the best, we all agreed, was the daddy poison dart frog carrying his offspring on his back.

The *Dendrobates auratus* is just one of the many thousands of special creatures God created. And like each one of His specials, this frog has its own unique, God-designed set of habits, its own unique make, and this one especially has a unique set of clothes. God certainly made him lovely, didn't He?

The poison dart frog— the highlight of our hike.

Black and White

And God created . . .

EVERY WINGED FOWL AFTER HIS KIND:
and God saw that it was good.

GENESIS 1:21

Chapter 14

BLACK AND White

My son Kenny and I were standing in the yard watching an approaching storm. The high, black clouds were piling up on the eastern horizon.

We called it the Dr. Seuss tree because of its funny shaped leaves and branches.

The front of the cloud bank was turning white from the slashing rain. It was 5 p.m. Then we noticed the buzzards coming in for the night.

For years I had known that a whole flock of Waslala's black vultures *(Coragyps atratus)* roosted across the field from our house, beyond the Waslala River and up in the trees on the high bank right behind the Río Lindo restaurant. Now several stragglers were flying in late. They were in a hurry because they were afraid they would get caught in the storm. They came in high above the trees and dropped like bullets, swooshing down several hundred feet to roost.

"Kenny, if we were standing there by the river, we could hear those buzzards drop. It sounds like a small bomber. You hear a roar, and you can even hear the wings whistle in the wind. One time a buzzard dove down right close to me. I wasn't expecting it, and it scared me badly. I jumped! I didn't know what in the world was coming out of the heavens at me."

Once the buzzards dove down to the trees' level, they slammed on their wing

The Dr. Seuss tree was full of black vultures.

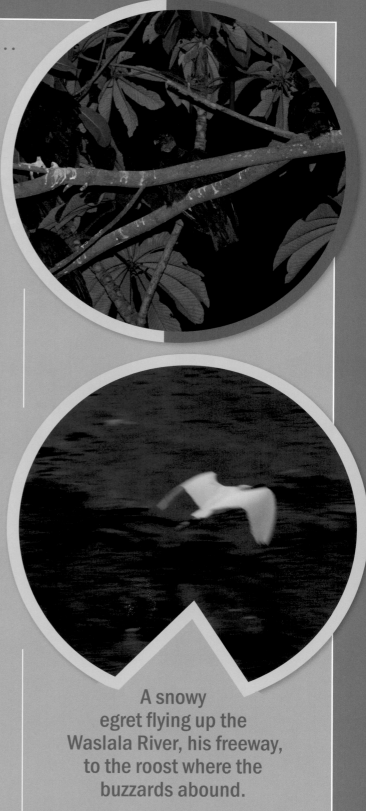

brakes and swooped right up into the trees. I noticed right away that most of the trees were guarumos *(Cecropia)*.

I could easily see why they chose these for roosts. Their trunks were straight and the branches mostly stuck out horizontally, making easy perches.

As Kenny and I watched the buzzards coming in, I was thinking of other things and only watching them out of the corner of my eye. Suddenly I saw some color contrast that caught my attention: snow white among pitch black. It couldn't be. I strained my eyes and saw the white flashes winging their way into the same treetops. I shook my head. Two snowy egrets *(Egretta thula)* roosting with the black buzzards!

Then I had a question for the egrets. *What in the world are you doing up there in the same tree with the buzzards? You are one of the whitest and cleanest birds in Central America, and you are landing in the same tree with the blackest, stinkiest birds in the world! What's going on, amigos?*

Kenny and I began watching the roosts evenings and mornings with our binoculars. Sure enough, several snowy egrets and even a pair of great egrets *(Casmerodius albus)* slept in the trees with the buzzards.

Then one evening we decided to go watch them up close. We went to the Río Lindo restaurant and asked for permission to watch the buzzards from their

A snowy egret flying up the Waslala River, his freeway, to the roost where the buzzards abound.

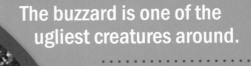

of the same crowd), as we say in Spanish. I think I'll preach a sermon with that title one of these Sundays."

"Yes," Omar added, "just like us here in this old sinful world. We rub shoulders with the world, but we are not of the same crowd."

Next Jacinto quoted from the Bible, " 'They are not of the world, even as I am not of the world' " (John 17:14). "In the world, but not of the world."

The egrets all slept in the upper part of the chilamate tree. The buzzards were beneath them in the surrounding trees. Black and white. Good and bad. On this earth, they always exist together at one given place. But they do not have to mix.

As we snapped the photos, the thing that made Kenny giggle and astounded me was how much the vultures fought. It seemed as if they were always fighting over the best perch. Kenny counted 146 buzzards coming in, so perches were scarce. Time after time a buzzard, all comfy on his perch, was chased away by a new one that was selfish and wanted his roost.

"Look!" Kenny hollered. "That buzzard

upper room, which was empty and close enough to get pictures. Jacinto set up the tripod and took the photos. Kenny counted the buzzards. Our native brother, Omar, pointed out the spiritual applications. I ordered tortillas with chicken and soft drinks and tossed in my own ideas.

"Look! The buzzards sleep in the guarumos and the egrets sleep in the chilamate. There are a few buzzards in the lower branches of the chilamate, but it looks like the egrets do sleep separately in the higher levels of the tree. Just like I thought, *juntos, pero no revueltos* (together, but not

not only chased the other one off, but he flew after him trying to peck him. As he did that, another buzzard took his perch."

Then two buzzards got into a real fight. Flapping, pecking, and fighting, they fell. They couldn't fly because they were too busy fighting. We held our breath as they fought their way toward the river below them. It looked as if they were going to be bashed against the rocks. Just before they hit bottom and certain death, they quit fighting and took flight.

Omar said, "If you watch buzzards, there is almost always some movement from a fight. They never hold still together. They are just like people who don't know God. They never have rest. They always go after their selfish ways, and that brings strife. Poor birds!"

"And the egrets don't fight at all," Jacinto added as he moved his tripod to another position for a better photo. "They are completely at rest. Each bird has his own perch and is satisfied."

"The main difference between the buzzards and the egrets is their diet," I reminded my crew. "Tomorrow morning the buzzards will head straight for the nearest road kill or dead cow. There they will breakfast on rotten meat. Ugh!"

"And the egrets," Omar smiled, "will fly upriver and enjoy a breakfast of fresh fish."

A snowy egret roosts above the buzzards. The gray one is an immature egret. Is that perhaps why he edges a little closer to the buzzards?

The wild music from the restaurant wafted up the stairs and assailed our ears. I knew that down on the floor below men and women were drinking and smoking. Here we were, discussing white and black birds, making spiritual comparisons, and eating wholesome food. Our hearts were happy and free. *"Juntos, pero no revueltos,"* I said again.

We finished our observations and photography. We finished our snack. It was time to go. It was dark now. Even the buzzards were almost holding still as they slept. Jacinto took a few last photos of the sleeping birds. The egrets were dazzling white when the flash caught them roosting. As we collected our stuff to leave, I was sure of two things. One, the egrets and the buzzards had taught us a good lesson on right and wrong. I couldn't wait until I could preach the message, *Juntos, Pero no Revueltos.*

Two, if I were a bird, I sure knew what kind I would like to be and where I would want to roost. I'd want to be clean, sleep in the top of the chilamate, and breakfast on fresh fish instead of rotten meat!

What about you?

I would rather roost with the egrets than fight with the buzzards.

WORLD

THE LITTLE ROOSTER
With the Hat

HE HATH MADE EVERY THING
beautiful in his time.

ECCLESIASTES 3:11

THE LITTLE ROOSTER
With the Hat

"Have you noticed the little roosters wearing hats?" Ezequiel, the little native chap walking by my side, asked as we ambled down one of the long gravel lanes in Mayjú, a big cattle ranch close to Pital, Costa Rica.

The owner of the ranch had real taste when it came to making attractive lanes. He had planted the native elequeme *(Erythrina fusca)* trees for fence posts. Then, unlike most farmers who trim the trees back every year, he had let them grow huge and tall. So large and tall were the trees' branches that they met high above us, forming the neat tunnel we were now walking through.

The elequeme trees were in full bloom. Overhead, among the leaves, we could see cluster after cluster of bright orange flowers that made the lane even more beautiful, like a long boulevard with millions of little lights to adorn the pathway. The trees were swarming with bees, hummingbirds, orioles, honeycreepers, and tanagers, and an oropendola even flew out up ahead as we

A rooster in the making.

interrupted his delicious nectar meal.

The tunnel floor we were walking on was also adorned. As the orange flowers matured, they fell off by the hundreds, so the road we walked on was sprinkled with thousands of flowers. Some were black and rotten, but others were still fresh and colorful. Most were in every stage between.

My little native friend hunched down and picked up the freshest flower he could find. "Do you have a pocket knife?" he asked.

A display of red-orange mini chandeliers.

"Sure, but what are you going to do with that flower?"

Ezequiel showed me the bloom. It had a unique shape, sure enough, and a long, broad, bright orange lip.

"Now watch," he continued as he took my knife and trimmed off the big orange lip, forming a neat little beak. Laying it in his open hand, he asked me, "What does it look like now?"

I almost burst out laughing. Sure enough, the cutest little bantam rooster lay there in his hand. He must have been a little bandit rooster, because he had his hat pulled down over his eyes as if he were participating in some dangerous holdup. Soon both of us were making roosters and laughing at their different poses.

Ever since, when February rolls around and dry season makes the elequeme trees bloom, I see roosters all around me. Then

Our front yard sentinel—an elequeme tree, full of grace and lots of sharing.

I trim off the orange lips and make the children laugh at the comical results. I love elequeme flowers.

But there is another large family out there that not only loves the flowers, but needs them. It's the birds. Dozens of species of birds visit the elequeme flowers daily. Appearing in February and blooming into April, the elequeme flowers serve as an important food source in nature. That's nesting time for most of the birds in Latin America. The flowers provide quick

> **Not only do the birds need the elequeme tree, but the tree needs the birds.**

energy for hard-working parent birds, or a direct source of nectar for baby birds such as hummingbirds or honeycreepers.

One morning I thought about the little roosters and went out and picked the very first flowers from the huge elequeme tree that graces our yard.

Not only do the birds need the elequeme tree, but the tree needs the birds. Notice how the flower is shaped. Do you see the arched shape that makes the rooster's tail? Do you see where the tail feathers stick out?

The tail feathers are actually the pollen stems. Notice that each stem has a little pollen pouch at the end. Right in the center of the stems is one stem that does not have a pollen pouch. It has a sticky tip. That is the stigma, of course.

The birds plunge their beaks up into the arched spout in search of the nectar. As they do that, their faces get well powdered with pollen. Then as they dive into the next flower, the powder will be deposited on the sticky stigma. Many feathered friends participate. Be it the big oropendola or the sweet little bananaquit, every bird that enters the nectar chamber scatters the pollen onto the stigma, and the elequeme's life cycle continues.

The elequeme tree is useful in many other ways. Ever since my family moved to Costa Rica from Virginia in 1968, we have planted live posts for our fences. We use elequeme mostly for the swampy areas. We trim a tree back and cut out approximately ten to twenty poles from the branches. These we replant. Often we just take our machetes and whack out a point on the pole. Then we slam it into the wet ground. In several years we have another pole-producing tree. With this system, it doesn't take long to surround fields with strong, cattle-proof fences.

The elequeme tree is also a legume. Because of that, the tree is a good source of nitrogen. The tree collects the nitrogen from the air through its leaves and deposits it into the ground through some little nodes on the roots.

Little roosters for children and nature lovers like me. Lots of nectar for the birds. Lots of pollen for the bees. Lots of fence posts for the farmers. Lots of nitrogen for the soil. Lots of beauty for the eye and for the soul. So much glory for the name that is above all names, our Creator, Jehovah God! Hallelujah!

A Repast
IN THE WOODS

I WILL REMEMBER THE
works of the LORD.
PSALM 77:11

Chapter
16

A REPAST
IN THE WOODS

Once upon a time, back when I was knee-high to Grandpa, we used to go to Grandpa's for Christmas. We children loved Grandpa's farm. The huge barn was filled with horses and cats. We played hide-and-seek in the haymows. The big black and white cows gave delicious, cold milk we'd dip right out of the bulk tank. The creek down in the meadow was perfect for swimming during the summer. But best of all was a winter noon in the living room, ready for the Christmas feast. Outside it was cold with snow on the ground, but the living room was warm and cozy. In the dining room a feast was waiting, with pumpkin pie for dessert. One time we had a gift exchange. I received a watercolor paint set which delighted me. But Mom's gift was the best.

Mom's gift that year was a big, flat, colorful box full of chocolates. Each candy rested in a little paper nest much like a cupcake's. There were all different shapes and sizes, and each had a different filling. But all were chocolate-coated and quite scrumptious. My favorite one to this day is the one you bite into and discover a sweet, red cherry in the center. Yummy a hundred times!

Way back then I had no

This happy cacao tree lives in the cacao capital—Waslala!

MY

idea where this delicious chocolate came from. Do you?

The cacao tree, *Theobroma cacao,* is relatively small. But wait, why don't I just show you? We raise cacao trees right beyond the pond behind our house. So come, follow me. First we skirt the pond, waving to the monkeys that swing on their island tree. Now we approach the cacao grove. Notice that the cacao trees are small and squatty with nice, big, oblong leaves.

The trees bloom year round. You don't find their flowers at the branch tips among the leaves as on other trees. They come right out of the branches and the very tree trunk. This is important because the fruit will get big and heavy and the thin branches would break. But since the fruit hangs on thicker branches, they can easily carry its weight.

The cacao tree's tiny white flowers are pollinated in the early morning by tiny insects that live in shady places like cacao groves. After being pollinated, the seedpods begin to grow. The fruit develops into a large pod that changes color as it matures.

First it's green. Then it turns red. And last of all it turns a bright yellow.

Green when they are immature and yellow when they are ripe.

Now let's pick a ripe pod and see what it looks like inside. We are about to find out where chocolate really comes from. We will even enjoy a little repast here in the orchard. We break the pod open by smashing it against the tree itself. See, it cracks open neatly, and we find a whole pod full of white seeds, each about the size of a quarter. Each seed is coated with

A sour-swe[et]
repast in th[e]
woods.

a white, sticky pulp. The stuff is actually good to suck on, but no, it doesn't taste like chocolate.

Now you taste it. Just suck off the white coating. It's sour-sweet, isn't it? But don't eat the seed itself, please. Although it's really the seed that makes your chocolate, it is bitter and inedible at this stage. Watch and see what the inside of the seed looks like when I cut it in half.

Your chocolate comes from that purple stuff in the seed. To harvest the cacao, we burst open the pods and gather the seeds. Then the seeds are fermented in their own pulp. After the fermenting stage, the seeds are dried in the sun. Then they are shipped to chocolate factories, where they are toasted and processed. Have you ever visited a chocolate plant? I have. There they will tell you what all has to be done to make that rich, delicious, brown stuff we crave and call chocolate.

The first to make use of the cacao beans are God's creatures.

Squirrels eat most of the beans in the wild. Cacao raisers despise squirrels! They simply chew open a pod and help themselves to the healthy, white pulp you just tasted a bit ago. The white-faced capuchin monkeys also eat the cacao fruit. Even some parrots chew holes in the pods and help themselves. Once the pods are opened, other smaller rodents and mammals get their share. If a squirrel opens a pod but doesn't clean up all the seeds, large fruit bats fly in to finish them up after dark.

I live in Waslala where a lot of cacao is grown. It's actually called the cacao capital of Nicaragua. The reason cacao grows

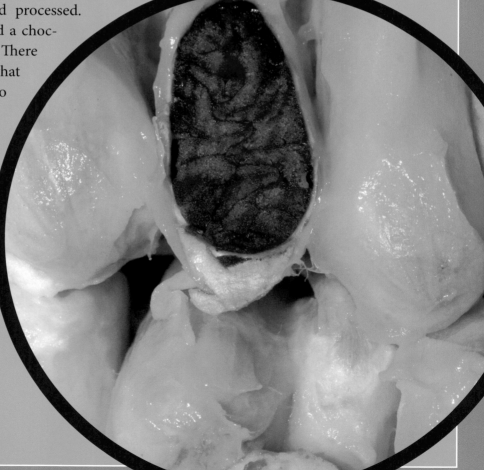

When you cut a seed open, you find this purplish meat that chocolate is made from.

so well here is because the climate is very tropical. We get lots of rain. Most years we get from 100 to 120 inches, which is perfect for cacao. Lots of rain and many hot, sunny days. That's Waslala.

No, we don't get many Hershey bars around here. But this is where the squirrels enjoy life, where the Indians first started roasting the beans years ago, and where tons of dried beans are shipped to the United States, Canada, and Europe.

There has to be a beginning to produce an end result, right? There has to be a hot, rain-drenched Waslala so that some dear mom, sitting in the corner of a grandpa's couch, can pop a chocolate-coated cherry into her mouth and sigh, "How delicious!" I'm sure she never dreamed what all had to take place before that chocolate ever touched her lips!

The dry seed pods the squirrels leave make excellent housing for mice and different insects.

The Invisible
Vine Snake

I THE LORD
have created it.

ISAIAH 45:8

Chapter 17

THE INVISIBLE
Vine Snake

The jungle is full of vines. They are a vital part of tropical flora. But sometimes these vines give you some unique surprises. Are you ready for one this morning?

Today you are lying on your back in a shady glen on the forest floor, right among the dry leaves. You rest your head on your arms and gaze up into the green canopy above you. All the birds flew away when you arrived minutes ago. Now you don't see any live creature among the tangle of brown vines above.

Suddenly you see a slight movement. Very, very slight. Something almost invisible comes sliding through the vines. It looks just like a vine, brown like all the rest of the vines up there. But this vine moves. It creeps straight forward, as stiff as a steel rod, and the tip looks much like the tip of a spear. A vine seems to have turned into a spear and now moves forward in extremely slow motion. You are

seeing a vine snake, *Oxybelis aeneus*, and are watching a typical drama of nature unfold right before your eyes.

Now the spear-like vine stops as if frozen. You suddenly notice that the spear tip has a tongue. Even the tongue freezes, stuck out in midair. For several minutes the snake is as still as a statue. Then the "vine" slowly moves forward again. Suddenly it explodes and in a burst of speed grabs a little green anolis lizard you hadn't seen because he looked too much like the greenery he lived in. The snake chews the struggling anolis, and in a minute the battle is over. The lizard now lies limp in

> That's one colorful but oddly-shaped head!

the snake's mouth, and the long, thin vine curls its body around, preparing to swallow its prey.

What we didn't see was that the snake chewed the lizard with a set of fangs in the back of its mouth. The fangs injected a mild poison that immobilized the lizard, making it easy to swallow.

Recently my hired man brought me a sack. As usual, I expected some interesting creature from the mountain behind our farm. I was not disappointed. When I opened the sack, a long vine-like creature began crawling out, lifting its strange, bullet-shaped head. What struck me as the strangest was how thin the poor fellow was. It looked as if he hadn't had any lizard for lunch for a long, long time. The next thing that surprised me was how long Mr. Vine Snake was. Almost six feet! Can you imagine a six-foot-long snake no thicker than your little finger? He displayed a comparatively big, strangely shaped head. Indeed the *Oxybelis aeneus* is a bizarre snake if ever you saw one.

When my hired man brought me the skinny snake, I had not read up on it. I did not know if it was poisonous or not. I didn't think it looked as if it was, but you never know. As the snake crawled out of the sack, he slid off onto the ground and suddenly was leaving before he had posed for photos. So I reached down and grabbed him by his tail. To my surprise, the snake swung around and lashed back at me with terrific speed. All my boldness and good intentions ran down the drain, and my hand jerked back as fast as a bolt of lightning.

"Are they poisonous, Dad?" my son asked innocently.

"I don't think so, but this skinny guy does strike!"

"Not only is he fast, but did you see his mouth?"

The inside of this fellow's mouth is a dark blue-black color. It gives him an awful, wicked grin and would scare off any brave hawk that thought to pick him up for breakfast. I can imagine a hawk's reaction to this snake's hideous strike.

If a vine snake bit you, it would not be fatal. If he got a good chew on you, the bite might swell and blister, and it might take a week to heal. It would cause you some minor discomfort, but it might well not be much worse than the scare he'd give you if he'd just bluff you with his big, gaping strike.

Now watch this. We turn the snake loose again in the same viny cove. The long snake slips up into the vines and simply disappears. This time he twists his body in among the vines, making their twining shape his own. Bingo! He has disappeared. No hungry hawk, no wise old weasel, no poor old opossum will find him for lunch! That's what God intended when He gave this snake his incredible camouflage.

Here Mr. Vine Snake is heading toward the vines.

The
Dogtooth Wasp

FOR HOW GREAT
is his goodness.
ZECHARIAH 9:17

Chapter 18

THE DOGTOOTH WASP

One day my hired man walked up to me with a mysterious look on his face. I saw right away that he had another surprise for me. "Pablo, guess what I found today on my way down the mountain."

"There is no way I could guess, Chevito. You always come up with new things in nature, but who knows what it is this time."

"I wonder if you've ever seen it before," he continued, keeping me in suspense. "Have you ever heard of a night wasp the color of milk?"

"Well," I answered, the hard drive in my brain working fast to pull up something, "yes, I have seen those wasps coming to the lights in our home. I always tell my children to watch out, because though they are not very aggressive, if they do happen to sting you, it hurts!"

"Have you ever seen their nests?"

"Yes, years ago in Costa Rica I think I saw some nests of these wasps. It's all so vague that I can hardly remember. They're flat, aren't they? The wasps sleep on the outside," I suggested, the memories coming back slowly. "I remember running into one or two when we macheted the high brush to plant beans. I'm pretty sure they have stung me; that's why I always warn my children—"

"Would you like to see a nest today?"

"Why, yes, did you find one?"

"I sure did. And it's not far at all. About a ten-minute walk."

Soon Chevito and I, along with my two sons, Jacinto and Kenny, were walking fast toward the highlands behind Waslala. We topped the first hill and Chevito stopped. Right off the main trail was an orange tree. Under the orange tree was a small bush. We crawled through a fence, and then Chevito pointed. On the far side of the bush among the gnarled branches hung a dogtooth wasp nest.

The first thing that impressed me was the order the wasps showed. I could only

A lazy, but orderly, batch of bums.

guess how many wasps slept there in the wide open. There were a lot. And they all perched perfectly in order, one right beside another, all the way around the nest. Because they are night wasps, they sleep all day long and search for food after dark. They look like a lazy batch of bums, sleeping the day away, right?

Quietly and carefully, Jacinto began to do what he does best—take photos.

As I stood and stared at the wasp nest, my brain was at it again. I was trying to figure things out. I confess that I didn't get very far until I read up on this marvelous creature whose scientific name is *Apoica pallens,* later.

First of all, this strange wasp nest does not have the normal cover wasps' nests usually have. I had never thought about the importance of the protective envelope around most wasps' nests. A nest without it would sure seem naked, wouldn't it? So why didn't the dogtooth wasps have it? Why was their nest just a hanging piece of a horizontal honeycomb-like thing where they raised their babies?

Now wait a minute. Do they or don't they have a cover for that private piece of honeycomb where the babies are grow-

ing? Yes, they do. Look at the photo. It's just not the papery cover I was expecting. But there is a cover, and a very efficient one too. A covering of bodies.

Maybe the inventor of the *Apoica pallens* didn't forget anything after all. What are the coverings for, anyway? For warmth. The envelope keeps the temperature just right for the babies as they grow. The coverings are also for privacy. The queen can lay her precious eggs in perfect solitude. And, last but not least, they are for protection. From wind and rain and from predators such as ants and other aggressive bees that can kill their brood.

Yes, the dogtooth wasp has a cover that is wonderful in every point. Can you imagine the babies getting cold under the blanket of so many fellow wasps? No, not even when the thermometer touches 61

Can you imagine the babies getting cold under the blanket of so many fellow wasps?

degrees Fahrenheit, as it did this morning. Those babies were snuggled deep under layer after layer of blankets. Oops! I mean bodies.

When the sun gets hot and the babies start getting warm, the wasps do several things. They back down the nest a bit and let some air through. Then anywhere from seven to a dozen wasps start whirring their wings. They work just like a fan. The whole nest cools off. The queen can go about her duties better, and the babies can grow! The wasps take turns fanning their home.

The *Apoica pallens* is a nocturnal wasp. God made them with eyesight that is much superior to other wasps. They can see in the dark. Just at dusk, almost all the wasps take a minute to stretch. That's a sight to see. All of a sudden, the whole nest is emptied. All two hundred wasps take flight and fly around the nest area to stretch their wings. But very soon most of them come back to protect the nest. The rest of the night the wasps take turns going out into the countryside to forage for food. More hunt when the moon is bright.

War is what the dogtooth wasps are best at. Most creatures that see a nest like theirs act very much like my son Jacinto. He must have had his share of stings when young, because when he sees a wasp nest, it immediately makes his hair stand on end. I always get the biggest bang out of his reactions.

The time came for the real photos. "Jacinto, now we need to stir them up a little so we can show people how they actually protect their nests. Get your camera ready."

"Daddy, you're not going to make them mad, are you? You already told me how hard they sting!"

"I'm not planning to get stung, son. It's daytime right now. They are really not aggressive at all in the daytime. It's at night

The dogtooth wasp is really quite a handsome fellow.

when you have to really watch out. These guys can't even fly fast in the daytime, and they probably can't see you very well, either."

Jacinto began setting up his tripod from a great distance, just in case.

"Come on, son, that's much too far away. You have to be close to get a good photo. Don't be afraid. They won't hurt you!"

"Daddy, I think you are going to have to take these photos," he snapped, dragging his tripod a hair closer. "I am not getting stung!"

Finally everything was ready. Kenny was giggling from a distance. Chevito had backed off too. Jacinto was poised at the camera, but by his stance I knew he would run before he'd ever snap a shot. I walked over to the nest with my machete. Hiding behind a bush, I slowly reached out with my machete and tapped the branch the nest hung on. Just a tiny light tap . . .

Nothing happened. But I still had to laugh, because that little tap made my son run!

"Jacinto, how do you think you are going to get a photo if you run before the bees are stirred?" I hissed, trying not to make the wasps angrier than necessary.

Jacinto sneaked back to the camera. I tapped again. A little harder this time. Again, the only thing that moved was Jacinto, who bolted again. Were these bees

These warriors are read[y]
for the battle even
in the daytime. "Don['t]
mess with us!" they
clearly say.

ready for war. Even I cowered and held very still behind the bush. But it was so very hard to keep from laughing as I caught a glimpse of Jacinto disappearing over the hill!

Colorful wasps that sleep all day in perfect rows. Wasps that fly around at night with wonder eyes that can see in the dark. Naked nests sheltered with a unique cover of wasps. A perfect blanket to keep a warm, cozy atmosphere. A perfect, orderly army to protect a precious queen and a whole nursery of tiny babies. When danger approaches, the nest explodes with well-equipped warriors ready for battle. They can fight on the land and in the air. Airborne helicopters, ready to insert a drop of their high-powered venom into their enemies, be they men or beasts. Everything made perfectly to fit the needs of this amazing little creature.

That sounds familiar, doesn't it? Yes, God did it again. Another lovely sample of the marvelous things God created for our enjoyment and for His honor and glory.

just a batch of lazy bums that didn't care about protecting their young?

"I know what, son. Use the timer. Then, once the camera is ready to shoot, I'll give the bush a mighty whack."

So Jacinto set the camera and backed off. First a light started blinking on the camera. Then it stayed on. I gave the branch a good solid whack. That did the trick. All of a sudden the nest exploded in a mighty whir. Some of the bees took to flight. All the others jumped up and got ready. The whole thing was a batch of angry wasps

THE LITTLE OPOSSUM WITH
Pink Ears

LIFT UP YOUR EYES ON HIGH,
and behold who hath
created these things.

ISAIAH 40:26

THE LITTLE OPOSSUM WITH
Pink Ears

Whenever we think of opossums, we usually wrinkle our noses, don't we? We immediately imagine a big, stinky animal playing dead and drooling saliva from its gaping mouth. But today I want to introduce you to an opossum that will smash that image forever. The Central American woolly opossum, *Caluromys derbianus*, is an opossum that will enchant you. If you don't believe me, let's just go meet him.

Some boys had brought me a mama woolly opossum with two babies that were old enough to have graduated from her pouch but young enough to still hang on to Mama and to nurse. I kept them in a cage for several days, but then I pitied the wilder mama and turned her loose. I decided to keep the naturally tame babies as pets. Sure enough, they were big enough to eat by themselves and seemed to be adapting

The Central American woolly opossum is indeed a beautiful animal. This one is just a baby.

to their new home.

One night my son Kenny and I were out taking our usual evening walk. Behind our house we have a coconut tree. I flashed my light up into its fronds to see what I could see. There was the mama opossum, sitting on a cluster of coconuts. Her cute face struck me again. Her fragile pink ears twitched nervously as she stared at my light. Her tiny hands clung to the coconut cluster. And her big brown eyes seemed to plead with me, "Bring me back my babies."

My heart melted. Soon Kenny and I were fishing baby opossums out of the cage. Holding one baby in my hand carefully, I stood up on a root cluster of an upturned tree. Balancing myself, I gently pitched the baby in among the coconut leaves. The baby opossum hung on for dear life and then began to search desperately among the fronds. In a matter of seconds, and with a happy squeak, the tiny baby leaped onto his mother's back. Then he plunged his head around to her belly, fishing for the teat. By then I almost had tears in my eyes, and Kenny actually did. The mama moved on back into the depths of the coconut fronds, and we went to get the other baby. We carefully pitched him into the fronds also, but since the mother had disappeared, we didn't know if he'd find her or not.

Several evenings later, Kenny and I were again out on our nature walk after dark. For some reason I was often flashing my light up into the coconut tree those days. Sure enough, we saw the most tender and sweet scene: Mama Woolly Opossum, her pink ears twitching as usual, and to our delight, two cute little faces peering up over her back. Their almost smiles seemed to say, "Thank you, sir!"

The Central American woolly opossum eats fruit, insects, nectar, and small vertebrates. They catch their prey with their tiny, pink paws.

Some scientists were netting bats once in Costa Rica. They had just netted a trophy, a Jamaican fruit bat, and he was squeaking up a storm. A woolly opossum nearby took the squeak to mean a free meal was available. He came sneaking through the trees in a hurry. Once he got to the wood's edge, close to the net, he jumped onto the only available post

near the net. He landed on top of the post, which happened to actually be a bareheaded biologist trying to untangle the bat from the net. Can you imagine the shock for the biologist? But now imagine the predicament for the poor opossum. The post he jumps onto begins to leap about and jerk at his tail . . .

Their almost smiles seemed to say, "Thank you, sir!"

Woolly opossums are more agile in the trees than most other opossums. They have dexterous hands and strong prehensile tails, well adapted for holding and gripping. That makes them very free and at home in the treetops, where they do a lot of their foraging. Nights they can be seen running around in the treetops and actually jumping from tree to tree.

In a study done in Costa Rica, several times woolly opossums were seen catching moths that circled around night flowers hanging at the edge of the canopy. The woolly opossum crawled out to the very edge of the branches. Once there, he let himself hang like a monkey, clinging to the outer branches with his strong tail and back feet. From that vantage point it was easy for him to catch the moths with his tiny fists and stuff them into his mouth.

Indeed, the Central American woolly opossum is another sample of God's creativity. It also shows us again His love for beauty. No one can deny that this unique little opossum is a beautiful animal. If it weren't quite so feisty and wild, it would make the softest stuffed animal to adorn your bed.

CANDY
Cane

HOW GREAT
is his beauty.

ZECHARIAH 9:17

Chapter 20

CANDY Cane

They really resemble candy canes!

Have you ever found candy canes in the jungle? I did once upon a time.

When I was young, I loved candy canes. Long and thin, curved at the end like a shepherd's staff, bright red stripes on white, so sweet and good to the taste. Yum! "May I have another one, Mom?"

Not too long ago we were on yet another hike in the jungle. We were climbing a mountain in Waslalita, back behind Waslala. I had a large, lively group along. I had found some super nice orchids. The jungle was virgin and the trees high and loaded with vegetation. The understory of the jungle was fairly clean as we worked our way around the mountain we wanted to climb. Suddenly a shout up ahead caught my attention. Jacinto yelled, "Dad, come check this out!"

I quickly made my way through the last stand of brush and sprinted up the trail. What I saw filled my heart with delight: a whole bunch of candy canes standing up-right on the forest floor. I had seen them several times before, though never so many. These were posing among the dead, brown leaves on the ground. It looked as if an elf had had surplus candy after Christmas and had randomly stuck them in the ground in this delightful miniature candy grove.

These candy sticks lacked the white stripes. They were bright red, except for the tips, which were done in brilliant white. Some of the sticks were short, maybe three inches high. Others were taller, up to twelve inches high. I knelt down reverently beside these strange plants and tenderly touched their slender stalks. What were they, anyway?

I e-mailed the photos to my friend Paul Kaufman. He found the information I needed. This plant is called Indian pipe. The one we are talking about today is not the white Indian pipe that grows in the United States. This is a tropical version of the same type of plant. Its scientific name is *Monotropa coccinea.*

What is this delightful plant, anyway? Is it in the mushroom family? No. Is it some kind of colorful root? No. Is it some kind of candy cane shaped fruit that fell off a tree? No. Is it a parasite that lives off other plants? Well, sort of. It's one of God's unique botanical creations. It doesn't contain chlorophyll, the green substance that most plants have in their leaves to absorb sunlight to make their own food. Because it doesn't generate its own food, it can live in the darkest jungle where the sun doesn't shine through. It draws nutrients from many different decaying organic substances it finds in the soil, but it doesn't rely directly on other living plants for nourishment like normal parasites do.

This plant never has leaves like most

Candy galore!

An Indian pipe in full bloom.

plants. Its roots branch out in many interesting directions and patterns, looking a little like coral found in the ocean. During its blooming season in February, the roots sprout this lovely flower.

Our Father loves dainty, lovely things, doesn't He? How many unique, intricate little things have you noticed in nature? For me, one of the sweetest and daintiest is the Indian pipe. This little plant speaks volumes about God's nature and His loving care for me!

As I slowly left the jungle grove, I glanced back one more time to say goodbye to my new dainty friends. As I saw how they bowed toward the earth, unheeding of me, I got the feeling they were bowing their little heads, worshiping their Creator. And indeed, by just simply doing His will for them, they were worshiping Him!

Here it looked like the flower was bowing, worshiping its Creator.

The Birds That Do
Everything Together

BUT ASK NOW . . . THE FOWLS OF THE AIR,

and they shall tell thee:

JOB 12:7

The Birds That Do
Everything Together

One day many years ago I was walking through the fields of Pital in Costa Rica. A drizzly rain fell, wetting the whole countryside, including me. I hurried home, thinking warm thoughts about hot coffee and dry clothes. As I jogged past a swamp, I saw a very tender sight. In spite of the rain, I stopped to enjoy the scene. On a low tree limb perched a whole row of coal-black birds with long, rounded tails and big, thick beaks. I knew right away that they were groove-billed anis, *Crotophaga sulcirostri,* birds belonging to the cuckoo family.

About eight or ten anis perched in a row on the branch, probably juveniles. Since it was raining and cold, they were all snuggled closely together, seeking heat. I was blessed to see their unity and closeness. One was cleaning his buddy's feathers and another was rubbing his beak on his sister's neck while they waited for the rain to pass. In my heart I knew where the secret of their unity lay.

When the mama and daddy anis are ready to seriously go into the nesting business between May and September, they don't work alone. They work to-gether as a community, two to five pairs per community. The anis choose very dense or thorny trees for their nests. This gives protection from predators and also provides a natural playground for their young. Everybody works together to build the nest, a bulky, open cup structure made with twigs. Then they line the cup with green leaf pieces.

The groove-billed ani's nest is not that large, but it is deep. This is important because there are usually anywhere from ten to fifteen eggs in each nest. The mamas never know whose is whose. The eggs seem quite large for the mama's size and are turquoise-blue covered by a chalky, white calcium layer.

After the mothers are done laying their eggs, they all take turns incubating them. After the babies are hatched, everyone pitches in to help haul the food. Can you imagine the job of bringing in enough grasshoppers and bugs for fifteen gaping beaks? But it's no problem; both the mamas and the daddies help.

Baby anis grow fast and eat a lot. By the time they are a week old, they crawl out of their nest and climb around on the edge

© Luboš Mráz/www.naturfoto.cz

The secret of their unity originates very early in their life.

and on small branches close by. Their feet are very large, and their claws have a wonderful grip to hang on for dear life. It's hilarious to find a bushy tree full of these little gnome-like birds that aren't even fully feathered, but are playfully crawling all over the place.

By the time the babies are two weeks old, they are feathered and learning to fly. They spend a lot of time in the tree they were born in, hopping and flying on short runs. By the time they are six weeks old, they are able to fend for themselves.

Many times I have seen a bushy tree where a clutch of groove-billed anis has just left the nest. As I approach the tree, what seems like hundreds of little black birds scamper in every direction. It always makes me laugh to see the circus. But I know that after I leave, they will group back together and be the community God made them to be.

Anis usually forage together in groups. These groups spend a lot of their time with cattle. That's why many people call them tick birds. It is not uncommon to see an ani jump up out of the grass to pick a tick off a steer's neck. But ticks are not their main diet. They follow cattle and horses because as cows and horses graze, they chase up all kinds of tasty creatures for the birds to dine on. So you can often see half a dozen anis hopping around in the grass at the cattle's feet. If you look closely, you'll notice they are picking up grasshoppers, crickets, worms, and other creatures.

The ani's Spanish name, *tijo* (TEE hoh), is a very appropriate name for this bird. That is its daily song. You can often see a

They all lay their eggs in an extra-deep, well-built nest.

© Lamp and Light Publishers Inc.

group of anis bouncing around in the grasses, singing their cheerful little song. Then as you get closer, they take off in a low, slow, laborious flight, their long tails streaming along behind like kites' tails, singing as they go, *"Tijo, tijo, tijo,"* looking for a branch to share with a friend.

What was God thinking when He created this communitarian bird? Isn't it true that we humans could use a good dose of groove-billed ani lessons? Oh, if our churches could be a little more like they are! When I see a branch full of anis, hud-dled together in friendship, I get a picture of a group of Christians clinging together in love. "Behold, how good and how pleasant it is for brethren to dwell together in unity!" (Psalm 133:1).

When I watch this comical, Roman-nosed, black bird demonstrating its daily antics, I know deep in my heart that it would be impossible for time and chance to come up with such a specimen. Could evolution come up with such an example of solidarity? No, not even if you figured on billions of years. Only God could come up with something so unique and marvelous. The groove-billed ani's life and habits clearly speak of the handiwork of our wonderful Creator, God!

THE BEETLE
KNIGHT

THAT THEY MAY SEE, AND KNOW,
and consider . . . the Holy One
of Israel hath created it.

ISAIAH 41:20

THE BEETLE KNIGHT

Have you heard of brave knights in shining armor? Legends tell about these knights and how they fought in days gone by, especially in England. They'd dress in shining metal armor and ride big stallions. They'd carry long lances and race straight at each other, trying to spear each other as their horses raced by one another. Because of the armor, it was very hard to make the spear actually penetrate the other knight's body. But oh, they could knock each other off! The knight who knocked the other rider off first won the contest.

Today I want to tell you about some feisty knights dressed in brown armor. I'm not talking about the knights of years gone by, either. They are real knights in Central America. These brave knights can fly. It seems they should be too heavy to fly, but they do

I introduce you to the majestic knight.

anyway. And as they fly they carry their armor and spears with them. When they land and meet a fellow knight, they are totally ready to fight. Their armor is hard—so hard that this knight's spear cannot actually penetrate the body of his rival. Though the spear cannot wound the fellow knight mortally, it can take him by surprise and knock him off his branch.

By the way, these knights often fight on branches. They seldom fight on the ground. They spend most of their time in trees. That's where they find their food. That's where they raise their families. That's just plain where they live.

Let's pretend we are in Central America. The rainy season has just started. It's evening and we are out looking for these brown knights. We stop at a streetlight on the outskirts of town and we wait. Then we hear a distant hum. A knight is coming in, flying low.

Our brave knight flying in to the streetlight is nothing else but the elephant

Here he comes, flying low.

beetle, *Megasoma elephas.* These beetles are so called because they are big, up to five inches long from tip of horn to rear, and because their armored heads look very much like an elephant's head.

Male elephant beetles' horns are used for fighting. The males fight each other during mating season. They fight to have the first rights over the female, which doesn't have a horn and doesn't fight at all. The males also fight to protect their feeding territory on their favorite trees.

The males often meet each other on a branch, head on. They have a terrific grip with their legs, which are equipped with mean hooks and barbs. When they grab onto your hand and you try to pull them

What a whopper grub! No wonder, when you see the whopper beetle he'll hatch into!

MY FATHER'S WORLD

off, they just jerk their legs in tighter and make you howl! To get them off, you must carefully extract each leg separately and hope for the best.

When elephant beetles fight, their spears can't actually penetrate each other's bodies. They are too well covered with brown armor, and their spears are blunt and have rounded tips. But they serve very well to knock the enemy off the branch and send him plunging into the depths below. At times one beetle actually lifts his rival off the branch and pitches him away. That's a sight to see! The falling beetle is not able to spread his heavy wing covers before he reaches the ground. But his armor absorbs the fall, and he soon buzzes his way home.

By far the biggest marvel about elephant beetles is the fact that they can fly. It's almost as incredible as seeing a real elephant fly. Before I understood their flying dynamics, I held a beetle in my hand and just shook my head. Impossible! He weighed about a ton! Of course, I'm talking beetle language. I mean, if you were a June beetle, and this fellow ten times bigger than you flopped on you, you'd be squashed! They actually weigh up to twenty-eight grams (one ounce). Think about it. For a beetle, that seems like a ton!

So I held the beetle in my hand and wondered. All I could see on the surface were the hard, short, shell-like wing covers coated with fine brown hair. I knew he couldn't fly with those. So I tried to pry them open to see what lay underneath. Might the secret be there? At first I couldn't open them. They were snapped shut with a tiny little latch. To open the latch, I had to first pry them slightly to one side. Then they popped open. Under the covers lay delicate wings that looked as if they were made of orangish wax paper. Somewhat like bats' wings, they had tiny veins through them that divided the wings into sections. The wax-like material was very light and transparent and yet extremely strong. Perfect for flying.

The next thing I discovered was that

> **" Under the cover lay delicate wings that looked like they were made of orangish wax paper. "**

these wings were twice as long as the short, hard covers. Now figure this out. If the thin wings are longer, how can he shut the stout covers without pinching and damaging the delicate wings? The solution is a marvel to see. The waxy wings are as neatly folded as my shirts when my wife packs my clothes for a trip. The wings just automatically fold when drawn in and are sweetly tucked under their protective covers. Fellow knights can smash against the side of any old beetle with their spears and his wings are totally safe. When the elephant decides to fly again, *pop!* The stout wings open. With a soft whisper and a unique display of delicacy, the long, orangish, waxy wings stretch out. The beetle flaps them, and away he goes.

When Mr. and Mrs. Knight want to raise a family, they must be very selective. They must choose a very, very big tree. And the tree must just be dying. It will not work if the tree is alive, nor if it is already rotten. After finding such a tree, mama beetle drills a little hole and lays her eggs in the freshly dying wood.

After the eggs hatch, they become hungry little larvae. These live on the rotten wood for a long, long time. They grow slowly and often shed their old skin for a new and bigger one as they grow. They will need to stay in the rotten tree for three or four years. That's why the tree has to be a big one. Can you imagine a small tree that would rot away in two years? What would the grub do once the rotten wood was gone?

If the elephant beetle is so big, can you imagine how big the elephant beetle grub worms must be? A friend brought me a set of whopper larvae he found in a huge, rotten tree. I kept them in a box full of rotten wood to see if I could get them to hatch out into beetles, but eventually they died. Though we didn't know for sure that they were elephant beetle larvae, they looked very much like they might be.

After the larvae develop into the pupa stage and then mature, the beetles burst out of the rotten wood

as adults and fly away to find some good tree with lots of healthy sap. The males fly to find other brown knights to battle with. Many fly to find a light to zoom around in the dark. But before long, the females fly to a huge rotting tree to lay their eggs, and the cycle continues. That's what elephant beetles were made for. That's their life. And though I'm glad I am not a beetle, I realize that they obey their Creator's will perfectly and in that way bring glory and honor to His great name!

A female elephant beetle folds her wings.

THE BOLDEST CREATURE
I'VE MET

FOR THY PLEASURE THEY ARE
and were created.

REVELATION 4:11

Chapter 23

THE BOLDEST CREATURE I'VE MET

I was at home one day, working on my computer, when the children ran into my office yelling, "Daddy, the dogs are running a strange, long, thin animal around the house. It's brown, and it runs slinking close to the ground."

Never too busy to see something new in nature, I sprinted outside to watch. Sure enough, our two German shepherds were going bananas. All I saw was a very slim flash disappearing into the swamp below our pond, the dogs after it.

"Who knows what it was," I concluded. "It looks like a long-tailed weasel, but I haven't seen a long-tailed weasel in a long, long time. Well, whatever it was is gone now. Gone for good. It won't come back with those two dogs running after it."

About fifteen minutes later my children ran into the office again. "Daddy!" they yelled. "The dogs chased the thing into the back porch!"

Again I ran. Sure enough, the dogs were whining outside the back porch. They knew they weren't supposed to come in, but oh, they wanted to! I realized the little creature, whatever it was, was somewhere in the house.

Our guest room lies right off the back porch, so I figured that's where the creature was hiding. Jeremy Yoder was staying in the room at the time and helped me search. As we entered the room, the first thing I noticed was a strong, musty smell. *Hmm, there sure is some stinky creature in here.*

The long-tailed weasel, *Mustela frenata,* sure is a handsome fellow.

For a fraction of a second Mr. Weasel stood still.

Sure enough, under the bed we could see the little animal dashing from corner to corner. Jeremy was barefoot and never dreamed his tootsies were in danger. But to Jeremy's horror the little animal flew out from under the bed and took a quick nibble at his toes. Jeremy was ready to get out of there, and I was ready to get in. (I had shoes on.) I grabbed a rug to catch the little weasel. I knew they had very sharp teeth, and Jeremy now knew it even better than I did!

In spite of all our care, the weasel shot out from under the bed and scampered out the door, though it was open only a crack. It fled into the back porch again,

me after it. To my surprise, the animal decided to hide in the bathroom instead of going out to face the dogs. I was so happy! I slammed the door and ran for Jacinto and his camera.

"Come on, son, we've got a great opportunity to get some good pictures of this weasel!"

Jacinto was wary, but he came. He didn't know what had happened to Jeremy, and of course I didn't tell him. He was barefoot as we slipped into the bathroom. He had the camera and I had a rug. I carefully closed the door behind us. *Gotcha, baby!*

There was no way the weasel could get out of the bathroom. We had him good.

Contemplating the drain route.

ing back and forth, I was constantly yelling, "There, son! There's your photo!"

But as soon as the camera was ready, the weasel was gone. It was becoming quite evident that he was not going to pose nicely for a picture after all. And then the worst thing happened. In one of his wild dashes from here to there and there to here, he unabashedly dashed out and bit Jacinto's bare foot.

"Daddy, I'm getting out of here! That guy bites! He won't stop for a photo anyway. I'm leaving!"

"Wait, son! Wait! Remember, if it's this hard to get him to hold still, then nobody else can get a picture of one either. This is the chance of a lifetime! Let's try one more time."

Jacinto tried a little longer. He got several shots, and then the weasel began doing something so unreal that we just stood and stared. He started running up the corner of the shower. Literally. The walls were as smooth as you can make plastered cement. But he propelled himself up with such force that he actually shot six feet up the smooth corner. I knew I would have to act fast, or he'd be a goner. In Central America our houses have a gap between the walls and the tin roof. He was about to escape right out under the eaves.

"Here I come, baby!"

I waited until he scrambled up the wall; then I lunged, my rug poised and ready. Before he could say "weasel," I had him. He squirmed fiercely in the rug, but my strong hands gripped him with all their might. Jacinto helped me unwrap him slowly. His

I flushed him out from behind the clothes hamper, and *zoom*, in a flash he darted into the shower.

I pulled back the curtain and saw him clearly for the first time as he stood still for an instant. His black facemask was outlined in white, giving him a very handsome look. I loved him on the spot, but he sure didn't love me!

I have never seen an animal as fast and as decided as this weasel was. In a flash he was gone into the farthest corner of the room, then back. He tried his best to find a hiding place. He even tried to go down the drain. Though our drain has a wide mouth, it narrows quickly to less than an inch. If it would have been big enough, I have no doubt he would have taken that route. Rac-

He's heading
your way,
Jacinto!

back part appeared first. And that, mind you, was unfortunate!

On either side of his exhaust pipe were two little protruding glands that were in full action. A gooey, yellow liquid dripped out, and wow, did it stink! I just about gave up and dropped him. I had almost seen enough. For sure I had smelled enough! There is no way to describe the awful stench. I can almost appreciate a skunk's smell. Especially from a distance. But this was so raunchy and horrid that it nauseated me. Not at all like a skunk's smell, it was more like . . . well, I give up. The only way I could make you understand it would be to catch another weasel and put him right under your nose.

After unwrapping my new friend, I started talking to him quietly. Maybe,

just maybe, he would quiet down. Jacinto kept hollering, "Daddy, what more do you want? Turn the rascal loose! He stinks too badly! Please!"

"Wait, son. We want some close-ups, don't we? Help me instead of yelling at me."

Finally we unwrapped him enough that I could get my bare hand around his neck. "Now I've gotcha! Here we go!"

Triumphantly I let the rug drop and held the weasel up for the whole family to see. He was not holding still like he was supposed to, though. His body twisted around and his sharp claws raked over my forearms again and again, drawing blood. Suddenly I sensed real trouble. He was working his neck out of my clamped fist.

I have held many animals by their necks. Angry monkeys. Frantic raccoons.

Fleshy boa constrictors. Even feisty alligators. But here was a tiny animal that was actually wiggling out of my grip. Never! It couldn't be! Frantically, I applied all my strength. I was going to choke him to death if I had to, but I was not going to turn him loose.

The weasel's neck is long, just perfect for a good grip. But its body is packed with tight, strong muscles. This weasel's neck, though long, was very hard to dominate. And the skin around it was loose and stretchy. I felt it coming before it actually happened.

"Daddy, turn him loose!" Jacinto shouted one more time. But it was too late. The little tiger had wrenched his head out of my hand and latched onto my thumb. I was stupid enough to still try grabbing him even as I howled, livid with pain. Then I felt the teeth crunch into my thumb, right through my thumbnail, as if it were tinfoil. Not until then did I scream and fling him off in one mad jerk. The weasel raced for the swamp again, the dogs after him. I was glad for the dogs' sake that they didn't catch him. Jacinto doubled over in laughter as he put his camera away. My one hand was gripping the other hand's thumb just about as tightly as I had held the weasel seconds before. I doubled over now, worse than Jacinto, actually moaning in pain. One thing is for sure, I will never again try to catch a weasel barehanded!

As I watched him disappear over the bank and into the weeds, I thanked God that He hadn't made him large. Can you imagine an animal as savage as that the size of a dog? Or a cow? I shudder just to think of meeting something like that in the woods!

Have you ever wondered why weasels are so long and thin? They are master burrow explorers. Can't you just see a weasel sneaking into a burrow, sniffing out a mouse or a snake? They have very keen senses of smell and hearing. He slyly slinks into the burrow, and if there is somebody edible at home, watch out!

If the somebody at home is not edible, and maybe is dangerous like a fer-de-lance snake, the weasel turns around and retreats in a hurry. But how can a weasel turn around in a burrow so narrow that only he and the snake fit? God gave him a very special backbone. It is so flexible that the weasel can roll upside down in an instant and then walk back over his own body, 180 degrees in a second!

Long-tailed weasels are also very clever and agile in climbing trees, where they search out bird nests and the tree's knotholes. There is actually hardly any place a weasel can't go. That's why he is so feared, far and near, by small rodents and birds.

God made many wild things. Some are wilder than others. It pleased God to put so much courage and savageness into the heart of the long-tailed weasel. And so, if it pleased Him, it pleases me too. No, I will never try to tackle one again, but I admire the creature very much for his courage and strength. And I admire the Creator who made him even more. Thank you, Father, for creating the long-tailed weasel! And especially for making him little!

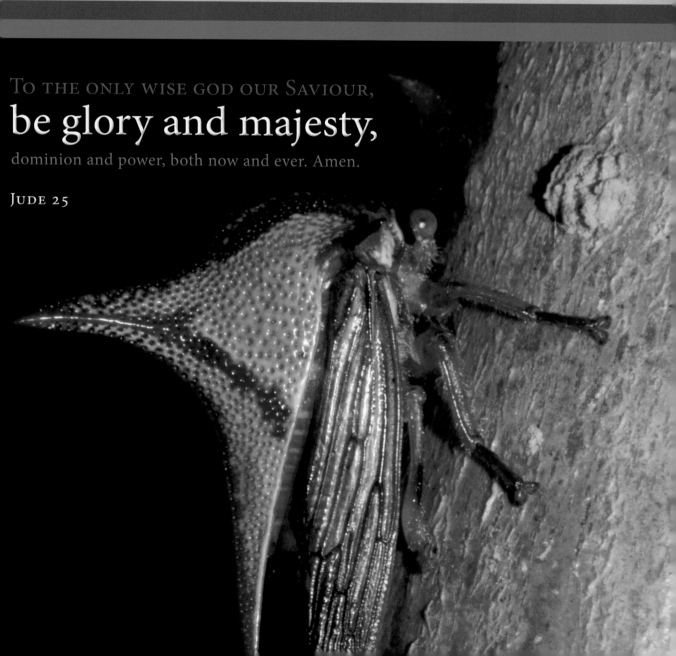

Thorns
that hop

To the only wise god our Saviour,
be glory and majesty,
dominion and power, both now and ever. Amen.

Jude 25

Chapter 24

THORNS that hop

One day we were traveling a cross-country, gravel road to a wedding in Jinotega in northern Nicaragua. I rode in the back of the Hilux pickup with a bunch of youth as we crossed a low mountain range and entered the drier, flatter terrain around the great Apanás Lake. As always, I had my nature-loving eyes wide open, watching for anything interesting in God's flora and fauna.

The area around Apanás Lake is cattle country with large grassy areas and rolling hills. Sprinkled through the grassy fields are lovely, green aca-cia trees. Their black trunks peep up out of the green grass and hold up their wide, shady canopies like lovely green umbrellas to provide shade from the hot sun.

Some of these trees' wide umbrellas stuck out over the road, and we drove under them as we meandered along, dodging

This acacia tree was the treehoppers' hiding place.

mud holes. Every time we drove under one of the shady canopies, I was all eyes, trying to see what the glade held that might be of interest. An orchid? A bromeliad? A bird's nest? A wasp nest? A lizard of some kind? But I was not really thinking of bugs . . .

A certain bug that looks just like a thorn and hangs out in thorn trees for disguise.

I was trying to straighten out my cramped back when we whipped under yet another acacia tree. As I stretched, my eyes followed a branch; then I saw them. *Oh, bugs that look like thorns!* I grinned to myself, remembering another of God's specials— treehoppers, *Umbonia crassicornis.*

I knew I had seen a cluster of them on the branch. *That sure would make a lesson for my nature book!* I mused. *But it's too late now. Besides, we are running tight with time to be at the wedding.* But I noted in my mind which tree it was.

The wedding was great. The couple seemed happy. I was happy to be there, but every now and then my mind wandered back to the acacia tree and the little treehoppers I had seen there. Would we stop on the way back?

After the wedding we almost drove home by another route. But I kept hinting that I wanted to go back the way we came. Yes, the

MY FATHER'S WORLD

road was rougher, but it was much closer. Finally, my opinion won.

As we reached the acacia area, my eyes scanned the roadside for the tree. It was right on the fence row. Right after a house with a huge rock in the yard. There it was! I banged on the roof of the pickup and hollered, "Jacinto, stop!"

Jacinto obeyed and answered, "What's up, Dad?"

"Photo time, son. There are some creatures here—"

"Come on, Dad. It's getting late," Jacinto grumbled, rolling his eyes. "Not again!"

Just like I wanted, Jacinto parked right under the tree for shade. The afternoon sun was beating down mercilessly, but that didn't matter. I was already standing on the rack above the pickup bed and had virtually disappeared into the thorny canopy, searching hard. "Get the machete," I yelled, trying my best not to tear my nice, white, long-sleeved shirt on the millions of acacia thorns. Someone found my ever-present machete. It took me a long time to find the hoppers. They weren't hopping at all. They were holding very still right beside the thorns that looked so much like them. But I knew they were there. By some strange miracle my eye had caught them as we had driven under this tree earlier. Why couldn't I find them now? Even as I searched, I knew what the prob-

Dear branch, hold the load!

lem was. My problem was their blessing! God had done such a good job of camouflaging them. Just about the time Jacinto was ready to jerk me out of the tree, I saw them. With a triumphant yell, I reached for the branch they were on, and Jacinto got the camera.

I cut the branch off very gently. I han-

> **They hopped, flew, and jumped. Because I was quick and ready, I caught three, and the rest disappeared.**

dled the branch as if it were made of glass, because I knew what the hoppers would do if they got too shook up. They'd hop! After a few photos, I started to collect several specimens to take home to check out better. As soon as I grabbed one between my fingers, bugs were everywhere. They hopped, flew, and jumped. Because I was ready and quick, I caught three, and the rest disappeared.

At home the next day, Jacinto and I took the little hoppers and placed them on an elequeme branch, *Erythrina fusca*. As we saw how they resembled the elequeme thorns, we shook our heads in awe.

"Son, not only would a bird have a hard time finding this hopper, but can you imagine the problem he'd have swallow-

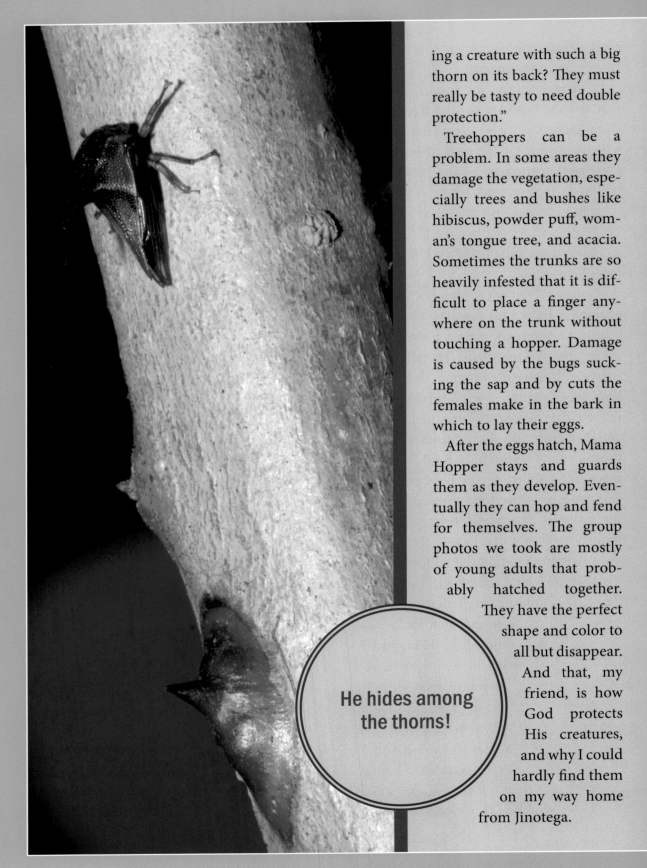

ing a creature with such a big thorn on its back? They must really be tasty to need double protection."

Treehoppers can be a problem. In some areas they damage the vegetation, especially trees and bushes like hibiscus, powder puff, woman's tongue tree, and acacia. Sometimes the trunks are so heavily infested that it is difficult to place a finger anywhere on the trunk without touching a hopper. Damage is caused by the bugs sucking the sap and by cuts the females make in the bark in which to lay their eggs.

After the eggs hatch, Mama Hopper stays and guards them as they develop. Eventually they can hop and fend for themselves. The group photos we took are mostly of young adults that probably hatched together. They have the perfect shape and color to all but disappear. And that, my friend, is how God protects His creatures, and why I could hardly find them on my way home from Jinotega.

He hides among the thorns!

MY FATHER'S WORLD

Chapter 25

IN SEARCH OF A STORY

FROM MY DIARY, JANUARY 2, 2008, 6:00 P.M.

The crickets' song provides our music tonight. The small brown bats have just started their jerky flights above us in the jungle canopy, making the place seem spooky.

My bed is a brand new hammock that is strung too low. My seat is already harassing a stump right below me. My nine-year-old son Kenny's hammock is hung right beside and a little above mine. My oldest son, Jacinto, twenty-three years old, has his hammock strung up just beyond Kenny's. Our roosts are so close we touch.

The mosquitoes are nasty, but repellent with extra strong Deet keeps them at bay.

· · ·

I wrote by the light of my little head-lamp. But I didn't write long. Words weren't enough. Besides, I was too tired and the night air was chilly. I tucked myself into my blanket as best I could and lay there like a caterpillar in its cocoon. But sleep was slow in coming. I lay awake and remembered . . .

My two sons and I had long wanted to get out into Nicaragua's wildest jungle to find

Our base where the girls stayed while we were up on the mountain. Domingo was friendly and opened his home to us.

stories for this book. I had dreamed and planned and packed, and now the dream had come true. We were in the wilds of a high mountain range called Peñas Blancas (White Rocks). Adventure in the raw.

My son-in-law had tried to warn me. "Pablo, are you sure you want to go camping on Peñas Blancas in January? Do you remember the time we tried it several years ago and almost froze?"

"Yeah, I remember," I had answered a bit too hastily, "but we weren't prepared. This time we are well prepared, and the weather has been great!"

So we'd driven up to the town of El Tabaco in our green Isuzu. Luana and Cynthia, my two youngest daughters, were along to help with the cooking. Chevito, my friend and hired man, came along as a guide and brought along his ten-year-old son Eliú. We were ready to climb.

First we hiked to Domingo's house at the base of the towering, jungle-covered mountain. We had arranged that my daughters would stay there for the next four days and help cook for us. Chevito and Eliú would haul food from Domingo's house up into the high jungles for my two sons and me, who would stay up there day and night. Domingo helped us find a native guide who knew the mountain range.

All the good guides in El Tabaco were busy picking coffee, and the only guide Domingo could stir up was Dennis, who was still half drunk from New Year's partying. By 2 p.m. we were ready to hit the mountain. Dennis ended up asking other bums to go along, all expecting pay, and we ended up with four fellows, all determined to help these crazy gringos reach the top.

The weather was perfectly clear and the air a bit nippy. As we approached the deep green mountain walls, Dennis announced, "The best way is to climb up that smaller mountain first." He pointed to a middle-sized mountain that jutted up right in front of a deep, canyon-like curve in the mountain range. On either side

The mountain seemed to loom over us.

snaked a deep, dark valley. "There is a trail. This way you will be close to the top when morning comes."

It sounded simple. Too simple!

"Is there water up there?" I asked, knowing how important water would be after a long hike and for making coffee the next cold morning.

"Sure, there are two creeks up there. You choose which creek you want to get water from."

We entered the dark, damp jungle and hiked up the steep mountainside. Kenny was always ahead with Eliú, climbing the slippery trail as agilely as a goat. I puffed along at the end of the train, excited about the great time we would have in the wilds that night.

Once we reached the top, the world below seemed distant. Tall trees towered over us, swaying slightly in a rising wind. "Here is your camping place," Dennis announced as he stretched his hand toward a nice stand of gigantic trees.

"Looks perfect," I agreed. "Where's the water?"

Dennis turned to me with a blank stare. "The water is down there, or down there." He pointed first to the right, then to the left. "You choose."

My heart sank. On either side of the saddleback were deep canyons. Way down below we could see the tops of the trees. I felt like jerking the earring out of his left ear, but instead I barked, "We can't go down there to haul water! We don't have any-thing to haul it with! We want to camp beside the creek. You promised us water; you take us to it!"

Shrugging, he reloaded his backpack, and we hiked down the steep bank, whacking with our machetes until we had a trail. It was so steep that we sometimes just sat on our haunches and slid to the next tree. Kenny and Eliú were delighted.

By the time we got to the bottom, we were not much higher above sea level than we had been before we'd started our climb. And we all knew we would have to hike right back out the next day.

The canyon at the bottom was just what

The smaller mountain in the center foreground is the one we hiked up the first afternoon.

we had expected. Two green walls on either side. A little creek rushing at the bottom. And not one nice, flat place to camp. I looked at Jacinto. He looked back at me. I shrugged. "Our creek behind our farm is nicer than this." But the evening was rip-

ening fast, and I knew we had to make the best of it. "Chevito, you go downstream and look for a campsite. Jacinto, you go upstream. I'll wait with the stuff."

We never did find the ideal camping place. But we found a nice stand of big trees forty yards up the bank from the creek. It wasn't exactly flat, but it would have to do.

In no time we had cleaned the place up and Chevito had strung the rope from one end of the site to the other. Next he hung a big piece of plastic over it and we tied the corners, forming a neat little tent. Then Chevito strung up the three hammocks under it, mine on the lower side, Kenny's in the middle, and Jacinto's on the upper side. We piled our backpacks in our hammocks so they would stay dry, and camp was made. I dismissed our four exasperating guides, thanking them kindly by way of apology for my earlier rudeness.

We wanted coffee in the morning, so we needed

> The canyon was nice enough as canyons go, but it didn't offer much in the way of campsites.

dry wood to make a fire. That was not easy to find in a damp tropical jungle. Just before Chevito left, he noticed a nice, dry post stuck in the soft dirt right beside the tent. "*¡Esto es una bendición de Dios!*" (This is a blessing from the Lord!) he announced as he whacked away at it with his machete. Soon he had a nice pile of dry firewood. He covered it with leaves so it wouldn't get wet if it rained, and he and

Eliú left for Domingo's house before it got dark. My sons and I were alone at last.

"Dad," Jacinto mused, "this is really neat. Just us two and you, enjoying the great outdoors . . ."

"Yes, sons, this is a dream come true."

I took out a frozen pigeon I had brought along for bait, cut it open, and laid it under a huge tree at the edge of our camp. I tied a string to its feet and tied the other end to the plastic right above my hammock. (I threatened to tie the string to my finger, but Jacinto was sure a jaguar would get the pigeon and haul me down the mountainside.) If an animal jerked at the pigeon, I would find out fast. Then I would shine my flashlight, and Jacinto would grab the camera and take some awesome photos.

We ate a snack of sardines and crackers. Then we looked at each other and wondered, *What do we do now?*

"Let's just go to bed," Jacinto suggested. "It's only six o'clock, but what else can we do? Sleeping will make morning come quicker." So I wrote in my diary and went to bed. By then it was so dark that I could almost reach out and touch the blackness. There, wrapped in my hammock, I was happy. No, we hadn't ended up at the top of the mountain. We hadn't even found a better place than the creek behind our farm. But we were camping in the wilds, and tomorrow night we would sleep on the top!

Before I went to sleep, I ran over the dangers we had been warned about.

Jaguars. Very few were left in the area, and even if one or two still roamed, they wouldn't come down into this deep ravine or much less attack humans. No, I was not afraid of jaguars.

Snakes. I had lived in the tropics and traipsed through jungles for most of my life. I knew that though there were snakes around, they seldom bit a human. No, I wasn't scared of snakes.

Getting lost. No, we had excellent guides, even if they were drunk. Besides, how could we get lost on a mountain where all the sides ran right down into a populated coffee area? No, I wasn't scared of getting lost.

This was great! No fear. I snuggled into my blankets and smiled.

It was after eight when Kenny first checked his watch. Jacinto was sure it was midnight. He claimed he hadn't slept a wink. I was cold. I pulled a heavy sweater over my t-shirt, long pants over my cutoffs, and socks onto my feet. I crawled back into my hammock and wrapped up again.

At about 9:30 we heard the wind coming up the canyon. First we heard a distant rushing sound. As the gusts drew closer, it became a roar. We were nestled deep in the canyon under tall trees, so we figured the wind would hardly bother us. The plastic flapped a bit, but that was all.

But the wind continued to rise, and when the roar of the full blast hit our trees, their tops swayed back and forth like twigs. A small branch broke loose above us and smashed against our plastic tent.

"What was that, Dad?" Jacinto shouted.

"Just a little branch. Nothing to be afraid of," I assured him. I remembered that the Bible spoke of the power of God in the wind. As I heard blast after blast ripping up the canyon, I thought, "Just how powerful is He?"

The wind swooshed through the opening of the canyon, and then, as if in a terrible crescendo, it galloped up the creek like some awfully angry beast. *Crash!* A giant tree went down somewhere to our left. We not only heard it fall, we heard it go rolling and ripping down the canyon wall to the creek in the bottom.

"W-What was that?" I stammered.

"That was a tree, Dad."

"That wind sure is getting strong, isn't it?" I added apprehensively.

"You'd better believe it!"

About half an hour later the next tree fell, somewhere to the right of camp.

"What was that?" Jacinto gasped.

"Another tree," Kenny stated matter-of-factly.

Every three minutes the wind came. We lay in our hammocks waiting to hear what would fall next. A third tree fell across the creek. Branches fell all around us. Usually just little ones, nothing to be scared of, but . . .

I hunched in my hammock, trying to stay warm. I had totally forgotten to shine at the pigeon or wonder about jaguars. The wind roared dreadfully; then it hit the treetops right above us. *Crack! Crunch!* My heart stopped and I trembled in my bed. I waited for the branch to smash into our camp. It didn't.

"What was that?" I sputtered.

"It sounded like a branch above us."

The next gust of wind roared into camp like a locomotive. *Crack! Crunch!* I was out of my hammock in an instant, yelling, "Boys, we're getting out of here, do you hear?" I was sure it was a miracle that a huge branch hadn't already ripped

> *Crack! Crunch!* I was out of my hammock in an instant, yelling, "Boys, we're getting out of here, do you hear?"

through the plastic and killed us all.

"But, Daddy," Kenny wailed, "It's cold. I want to stay in my hammock."

"No way, son. A big branch could fall any minute. Let's go."

We gathered in a huddle under the huge tree beside our camp. The wind came again, stronger than ever. This time it sounded as if the cracking came from the base of a large tree right beside the giant we were hiding under. It actually made the earth under us tremble. We fled our camp. We weren't sure what was breaking, but we didn't want to be there to find out.

We didn't want to go down to the creek where the falling trees ended up, so we scrambled up the mountainside like three armadillos, sometimes on our hands and knees, slipping and sliding, but never moving fast enough. I had remembered to grab the machete, and we each had a flashlight and a blanket. We found a palmetto grove far enough from camp to feel safe. No big trees towered over us here, just small trees and palmetto branches that whipped in the wind every time it bellowed up the draw.

Eventually we lay down on the soggy ground under the palms and tried to sleep. But it was wet and cold and the ground wasn't nearly flat. We tossed and turned for what seemed like hours. Finally, we hiked back down the mountain to get our hammocks. We left Kenny just far enough from camp to feel safe but close enough to watch our lights. "If the wind rises, Kenny, and you hear a cracking sound, you run that way." I pointed back up the hill toward the palmetto grove. Then Jacinto and I swooped into camp. I ran to the tree I suspected and whacked it with my machete. Sure enough, the tree was rotten and leaning right over our camp. We loosened our hammocks and escaped up the hill before the wind rose again.

After searching and deliberating, we finally strung up our hammocks just over the rise from our former campsite. The bank was steep, but the hammocks hung level. It was 2:30 a.m., and we were dead tired. The wind died down, and sleep came slowly but surely.

At five o'clock it was still dark. The wind was rising again. Kenny and I were fast asleep, but Jacinto was worried. He was sure the big tree down by our campsite was leaning toward us and would either crush us or bring down a host of other trees on us. The tree started breaking again. The first crack got Jacinto on the mark. The

second got him set. At the third and loudest crack he was beside my hammock yelling, "Dad, let's get out of here!"

So for the second time that night we took to the hill. We found the palmetto grove and spent some more time curled up in our blankets. After daylight we hiked down to the river. We sat on rocks and waited for Chevito to bring us breakfast. Then Jacinto asked the question that was on all our minds: "Dad, what about tonight?"

"Well, two things are for sure. One, the top of the mountain is going to be worse than this. And two, I'm not sleeping one more night in this wild, dangerous place."

Chuckling, Jacinto agreed that the only sane thing was to sleep at Domingo's place. Kenny wailed, "But Daddy, I love to sleep in my hammock! Let's sleep up here for at least one more night."

Though I was tickled pink to see that our night hadn't dampened my little son's spirit, I soon convinced him that we would explore the mountain during the day but head for a safer spot to spend the night.

Soon one of our guides arrived at camp, so we joined him. The wind had died down and we felt fairly safe. Jacinto and the guide got a fire going with Chevito's firewood, and after a bit we had a pot of black coffee brewing. Soon Chevito and Eliú arrived. We told them our night's story, and together we analyzed the rotten tree that hung over our camp. It had broken at the base and halfway up and was leaning far enough that it was trapped between two smaller trees, suspended in a tangle of jungle vines. I shuddered as I realized that the two trees were the very ones our hammocks had been tied to. If the rot-

firewood we had found so handily the evening before. Our guide wasn't impressed. "Don't you see what that was? A dead branch fell headlong from your tree and buried itself two feet in the soft soil."

I stared at what was left of the black branch. It was almost as big around as Kenny's waist. The evening before it had stood there, a clear warning, four feet high. I had grabbed and jerked at it and wondered what it was doing there, planted just like a fencepost. Now I thanked the Lord under

What was left after we cut our firewood from the rotten branch that once upon a time had dropped from the treetops.

ten tree had fallen, it would have crashed right smack into our camp.

Chevito handed us a blue plastic bucket. "Here's your breakfast," he announced. Three big plates of food were stacked in the bucket. Three huge tortillas per plate. Rice and beans. Egg and potato patties. And a big bottle of orange juice. We gathered in a huddle to pray and dug into the best breakfast we had ever eaten.

As we ate, someone mentioned the dry

my breath that not more branches had dropped in the night and buried themselves two feet deep into whatever was there.

We spent the day hiking around the canyon on a higher level. At one point our guide claimed we were only half an hour from its wild peaks. But it was raining softly, and we were bushed. Our guide took us to a cave where we were able to catch and photograph several vampire bats. Along the mountain trail we found some lovely red and white Indian pipes like you read about in this book. We enjoyed the birds, took in majestic views, challenged steep mountains and cliffs, appreciated all kinds of interesting vegetation, and all in all had a spanking good day.

No, we didn't see any jaguars or quetzals as we had hoped. We didn't find a snake or a porcupine. We didn't even find one story for the book, except this one! But when in the late afternoon we finally reached Domingo's place and looked back up into the dark, wind-whipped highlands of Peñas Blancas, we knew we had savored an adventure never to be forgotten. And though we all agreed we would never want to go

through a night like that again, we would not have missed it, either!

God in heaven often looks down upon His creatures. He sees when adventurous hearts are slightly bigger than the adventurers' brains. He watches them strike out courageously, even if a bit senselessly. Then He smiles, and His winds rise, and His trees crack under His blast. But he reaches down and strengthens His vines and protects His helpless, frail children. And in spite of all odds, the adventurers come out unscathed, shouting that they had a wonderful time, and especially praising their Creator!

Tropical plants adorned a waterfall we found up in the canyon.

143

I hope that at the end of this book you are as excited about nature as I am. God's creation is just plain awesome.

I am writing this conclusion from a place called Zapote Kum. As a family we volunteered to serve at this back-in mission for two months. The house we live in is perched on a hilltop and surrounded by rolling green hills, several huge trees,

est grass. They come in all sorts of shapes and sizes, but all are steep and rugged.

When I get up in the morning and tiptoe out into the yard and see God's world in Zapote Kum, I feel so small. I know I am only a tiny speck in God's vast universe, and I am overwhelmed as I drink in all the beauty. Then I remember that we must always worship the Creator and not the creation. The Bible says that the unrighteous worship and serve created things rather than the Creator, who is forever praised (Romans 1:25).

When I think of this verse I remember the photo my son took the other day. Billowing clouds just beginning to reflect the sunset grace the background. A green jungle-covered mountain rises in the distance. Creation in all its glory. But in the foreground stands an old rugged cross. For our God Jehovah, some things are even more important than the lovely things He made. Like what He did for us in Christ Jesus. It's because of that most important work on the cross that we can know God and be His children. And because of the cross, all nature and all of life makes sense. That's why, when I get up early in the morning and tiptoe out into the yard, I can enjoy God and His creation. My relationship with the Creator makes nature even more special, and the beauty and wonder of the things He has made draw me even nearer to Him.

May it be so for you.

and a big corral. Beyond that lies an awesome valley where we can watch immense storms develop and then drench the land.

The sunsets and sunrises in this place are too lovely for words. Surrounding this paradise are unique mountains, some covered with jungle and some with the green-

Pronunciation Guide

Apanás	ah pah NAHS
Bernal Rodríguez	behr NAHL roh DREE gehs
Cerro Blanco	SEH roh BLAHN koh
Chevito	cheh VEE toh
Chico	CHEE coh
chilamate	chee lah MAH teh
Domingo	doh MEEN goh
El Tabaco	ehl tah BAH coh
elequeme	eh leh KEH meh
Eliú	eh lee OO
Ezequiel	eh seh kee EHL
guaba	goo AH bah
guapinol	gooah pee NOHL
guarumo	gooah ROO moh
Jacinto	hah SEEN toh
Jinotega	hee noh TEH gah
La Tigra	lah TEE grah
La Tirimbina	lah tee reem BEE nah
machaca	mah CHAH cah
Managua	mah NAH gooah
Mayjú	mah ee HOO
orquídea cara de mono	ohr KEE dyah CAH rah deh MOH noh
Papayo	pah PAH yoh
Peñas Blancas	PEH nyahs BLAHN kahs
Pital de San Carlos	pee TAHL deh sahn CAHR lohs
Puerto Viejo de Sarapiquí	poo EHR toh vee EH hoh deh sah rah pee KEE
Reserva Biológica la Tirimbina	reh SEHR vah bee oh LOH hee cah lah tee reem BEE nah
Río Lindo	REE oh LEEN doh
Río Toro	REE oh TOH roh
San Carlos	sahn CAHR lohs
Sarapiquí	sah rah pee KEE
Volcán Tenorio	vohl CAHN teh NOH reeoh
Waslala	wahs LAH lah
Waslalita	wahs lah LEE tah
Yaró	yah ROH
Yesenia	yeh SEH nyah
Zapote Kum	sah POH teh koom

ABOUT THE PHOTOGRAPHER/AUTHOR

Once upon a time he was little, but now he's bigger than I am. I used to be able to teach him things I knew, but now, when it comes to running cameras and computers, he leaves me trailing in the dust with my eyes full and sneezing. His name is Jacinto, and I'm proud to say he's my son!

Over a year ago Jacinto married his little Kendra and moved up on the hilltop behind our house. It's truly a photographer's paradise. He edits my books and any other books he gets his hands on. But if you really want to see him happy, turn him loose in the wild with his camera. Jacinto and I make a team. I write the books, and he takes the pictures and edits the manuscripts.

Now my "little boy" is co-minister with me in our church in Waslala, Nicaragua, where he and his wife have been commissioned to start a new church in remote Zapote Kum. But the best thing about my little son who got big is that he is one of my best friends! God bless him!

As for me, I serve the Lord with my wife Euni and our family in Waslala, Nicaragua, where we have been involved in evangelization, church planting, and ministry since 1995. My interest in nature began when I was a boy. My family moved to Costa Rica when I was ten, and my nature-loving heart rejoiced in a whole new world of birds, animals, flowers, and trees. I enjoyed writing too and kept journals of all my discoveries.

I still enjoy exploring nature as much as I did when I was a boy, and I still love writing about God and His wonderful creation. I also enjoy hearing from people who read what I write. I can be contacted by e-mail at emailmeinnic@gmail.com or written in care of Christian Aid Ministries, P.O. Box 360, Berlin, Ohio, 44610.

To learn more about God's work in my family, you'll want to read *The Long Road Home, Angels Over Waslala,* and *Angels in the Night,* all available from Christian Aid Ministries.